ALL THE POWERFUL INVISIBLE THINGS

A SPORTSWOMAN'S NOTEBOOK

GRETCHEN LEGLER

SEAL PRESS

Cover and text design by Clare Conrad
Cover photographs by Craig Borck

Acknowledgments:
The following essays were originally published in the following publications: "Border Water" in *Uncommon Waters: Women Write About Fishing,* edited by Holly Morris (Seal Press, 1991); "Fishergirl" in *A Different Angle: Fly Fishing Stories by Women,* edited by Holly Morris (Seal Press, 1995); "Gabimichigami" and "Gooseberry Marsh" in *Indiana Review 16.1* (Spring 1993); "Puerto Peñasco" in *Hurricane Alice* (Fall 1993); "Wildflowers" in *Indiana Review 14.3* (Fall 1991); and "Wolf" in *Another Wilderness: New Outdoor Writing by Women,* edited by Susan Fox Rogers (Seal Press, 1994).

Library of Congress Cataloging-in-Publication Data
Legler, Gretchen.
     All the powerful invisible things : a sportswoman's notebook / Gretchen Legler.
1. Legler, Gretchen—Biography. 2. Women authors, American—20th century—Biography. 3. Outdoor recreation for women—West (U.S.) 4. Lesbian—United States—Biography. 5. Outdoor life—West (U.S.) I. Title.
PS3562.E39Z463   1995   814'.54—dc20   95-14524

Printed in the United States of America
First printing, September 1995
10 9 8 7 6 5 4 3 2 1

Distributed to the trade by Publishers Group West
Foreign Distribution:
In Canada: Publishers Group West Canada, Toronto, Ontario
In the U.K. and Europe: Airlift Book Company, London, England

ACKNOWLEDGMENTS

Our stories are never wholly our own. The essays in this collection come from crossing places where my life has intersected the paths of many other generous, alive, beautiful and flawed human beings. There are also the landscapes, and of course the animals, whose spirits I feel lucky to have met.

I especially thank the members of my family and Craig for their individual willingness to lend their part of this long story to me. I honor them for their graciousness in supporting me and this work, despite its sometimes painful content. To all of the others whose names or stories appear here, no less a grateful thanks.

Just as our stories are never entirely our own, our creative endeavors are also shared. I owe much to my writing mentors and supporters in English and Creative Writing at the University of Minnesota: Charles Sugnet, Madeline Sprengnether, Toni McNaron, Paulette Alden and Patricia Hampl.

Members of several writing groups saw these essays in every stage of creation. Thanks to Mary Petrie and others in the "Riverside Group" for their careful attention to my work from the beginning. Thanks to Barrie Jean Borich, Janice Paynick, Terri Whitman, Elizabeth Mische John, Joyce Sutphen, Cheryl Strayed, Anett Jessop, Jeanne Swope, Brian Felland and others for their sustained, focused writerly wisdom and comradeship. For all the other friends who read drafts and provided suggestions and praise, my sincere thanks.

Grants, prizes and writing time provided by several organizations helped make this work possible and gave me early encouragement. Thanks to Judith Barrington at Flight of the Mind, Joan Drury at Norcroft, and the University of Minnesota Center for Advanced Feminist Studies.

Those who supported this work by being the finest of friends know who you are. I extend myself to you.

Ellen Levy, Kelly Craigmile, and Susan Johnson saw these essays through to their exquisite end. Their energy, their love and their talent have been a priceless gift. A special thanks to Joan James for her keen readerly eye and joy for life.

Finally, thanks to Holly Morris and others at Seal Press for taking up this project, for shaping it, for pushing it along, for devoting to it so much of their humor, intelligence and skill.

CONTENTS

ALL THE POWERFUL

INVISIBLE THINGS

BORDER WATER

THE RAINY IS A GREAT, wide, slow-moving river that runs from east to west, through forests and farms, at the top of Minnesota, separating the state from Canada. Because it is a border water, you can fish the river in early April, after the ice has gone out, a full month before you can fish inland waters.

Craig and I are on our way to the Rainy to fish for spring walleyes. "It's hard to imagine," he says as we drive along the Minnesota side of the river, looking across at the brown grass and the farms on the opposite bank, "that just over there is another country." On both sides of the river there are brown grass and trees and red barns and silver silos. It looks the same. Over there, Ontario, rust-colored grass and trees. Over here, Minnesota, rust-colored grass and trees. It is hard to imagine. But it is a different country, a place boys rowed across to in rickety boats to avoid being sent to Vietnam. It is beautiful and open and wild along the river. Behind the trees on the Canadian side there is a railroad track, and occasionally a freight train roars by, speeding as trains do only in the country.

We have purchased Canadian fishing licenses so that we can fish both sides of the river. We have also purchased three dozen minnows and salted them down. You can use Minnesota minnows on the Canadian side as long as they are dead. If you want to use live minnows on the Canadian side, you must buy them in Canada. But you can't cross the border checkpoint at International Falls or Baudette with live minnows, so if you want to legally fish with live minnows on the Canadian side, you must launch your boat in Canada, which means you must patronize the Canadian resorts, of which there are none on this stretch of the Rainy.

As Craig drives, I read the fishing regulations. I turn to the fish consumption advisory. It says that on the Rainy River between International Falls and Lake of the Woods no one should eat more than one fish meal per month of any size of any species caught there, especially if you are pregnant or plan to be, ever, or are nursing, or plan to, ever, or if you are less than ten years old. For years the Boise Cascade paper mill at International Falls has dumped dioxin, mercury and other poisons into the river. The large fish in the river taste slightly metallic. Two decades earlier, the river was a slime pit of stinking paper pulp, great pods of which would burp open on the water and emit putrid gas. Now at least, old-timers say, the visible pollution is gone, the water is clear and there are fish here again.

"Why are we coming here if all we're doing is poisoning ourselves?" I ask Craig. But I know why, of course. We are going to be out on the first open water of the season and we are going to fish. That means sitting still and thinking and maybe reading if I get bored, talking quietly about important things, watching the sky, seeing an eagle fly over, a few mallards whiz upriver, the brown grass on the bank, the current bringing big sticks past.

Craig says, "Why doesn't someone sue Boise Cascade's ass? I don't know how they can get away with polluting like that."

This is a trip Craig and I have taken for four years in a row. "These traditional things are important," he says. "It's important to have a history of experience together."

His eyes are on the road, and I watch his profile: a sharp forehead and nose, cheeks, eyes, and lips framed by a closely trimmed gray-black beard, and a sloppy, sweat-stained gray Stetson. He looks very young to me, and slightly naive; like a Boy Scout still. I agree with him about the importance of ritual. We fish rainbow trout in the fall at Benjamin Lake for two weekends. We walk the logging trails around Blackduck for grouse. Then there is the season for ducks and geese near Thief Lake. Then we hunt deer in the woods of northern Minnesota to fill our freezer for the winter.

When it snows we ski, and when the lakes freeze we fish through the ice for crappies. In the spring comes the Rainy River, then walking in the woods for morel mushrooms, then summer walleye fishing on big, smooth lakes. Our year together is spent in these ways. It is what we do.

But I am uneasy about the trip to the Rainy this time. For one thing, it is always difficult, physically demanding. To load and unload a boat, walk up and down the steep, slippery hill from the river to camp in heavy boots, all is wearing on my body. I get tired. I worry that I am becoming soft and weak. The weather is always unpredictable. One year as Craig and I bobbed in the current, jerking our minnow-baited jigs up and down, snow fell and ice chunks floated past us. Another year it was so warm we fished in shirt sleeves. This year the weather is in the middle, sunny and cold. But still there is the physical work of it. Hauling. Endless hauling.

But I know my unease has less to do with this, and more to do with the first year we came here. The fishing was so good that year that the river was a solid mass of boats, gunnel to gunnel, bow touching bow, stern to bow, stern to stern. It was sunny, and everyone was having a wonderful time, lifting huge fish from the muddy water, smiling, laughing, weighing the fish, some putting the big ones back, but others keeping stringers of seven-pound fish, whole stringers of fish that would not even taste good, fish that would taste like metal.

At the boat ramp, men milled around, laughing and smoking cigarettes and drinking beer and pop. They were drunken, overloaded, dangerous. The wives and girlfriends of the fishermen stood with poodles on leashes, holding children by the hand, taking pictures of the great catches of fish. The fish-cleaning house was packed, and there was a line outside. The garbage cans in the fish house were overflowing with guts and the orange eggs of the huge spawning female walleyes. Fish heads with shining black eyes flowed out onto the ground. Flies buzzed around.

I was as giddy as all the rest with our success. Every cast brought in another huge green and gold fish, tugging at my line, twisting and spinning in the water, curved gracefully in the landing net, all muscle. We didn't keep them all, only the small ones. And we only kept our limit: twelve.

~

We camp this year, as always, at Franz Jevne State Park on the river. It is not much of a park; a few dirt pullouts and two outhouses. The roads are winding and muddy, and the park is dark. Our small camp is in the middle of tall evergreens. I feel vaguely gloomy. Surrounded. It is dim and cool, early evening, and the men around us in other camps are lighting lanterns, starting campfires, firing up cooking stoves. I smell fish and onions and wood smoke. I see shadows moving behind the canvas walls of tents. I hear muffled, rough voices. I am the only woman here.

In the women's outhouse I sit down to pee and look at the wall in front of me. There is a crude drawing in thick black marker of a woman's vulva, a hairless mound, lips open wide, folds of flesh deep inside. The rest of the body is absent. There is no head, no face, no eyes, no mouth, no arms or legs. Just this one piece, open and dripping, as if it were cut off with a cleaver and set apart. I imagine it wrapped up in white butcher paper, the kind we'll use to wrap the walleyes we catch here. "I want to fill your pussy with a load of hot come," the writing above this picture says. Cold air is blowing up from the pit below me, hitting my warm skin. My muscles shrink. On another wall is an erect penis, huge and hairless, drawn in the same black marker. The head on the penis looks to me strangely like the head of a walleye with its gills spread wide. There is no body attached to the penis either, just a straight vertical line from which the organ springs. "I want to fuck your wet pussy. Let's meet." is scrawled next to it.

I am suddenly terrified and sickened. I hear a threat: *I want to rape you; I want to dissect you.* I can't pee anymore. The muscles of my stomach and thighs have pulled into themselves protectively, huddling. Between my legs now feels like a faraway cold world, not a part of me. I yank up my long underwear and wool pants, getting shirt-tails tucked into the wrong places, and leave with my zipper still down, happy to be outside. As I walk back to our camp I look over my shoulder and left and right into the woods. I wonder if it was that man, or that one, or that one, who wrote this violence on the wall. I am out of breath and still afraid when I tell Craig all of this. I tell him it makes me want to run and it freezes me in place. My voice is wavering. He tells me it is in the men's outhouse, too: a picture of another naked, dripping vulva and the words, "This is my girlfriend's pussy." I ask Craig, "How would you feel if in the men's john a woman had written 'I want to cut your dick off' or 'This is my boyfriend's cock'?" I want to know if this would scare him, too. He says, "I'd watch out."

We are anchored in the current, our jigs bouncing on the bottom of the river. The river is wide and powerful and brown. It smells like cold steel. Craig wonders aloud why in all this water the poison and its smell do not dissipate. We are not catching many fish, but some. Crowded around us are men in boats. This is a good spot, on the Canadian side of the river, and the boats push together here. There are no other women on the water. Only men with other men. Some are drinking Diet Coke and munching on crackers as they wait for fish to bite. Others are swigging beer, cracking jokes, laughing. Cigar and cigarette smoke wafts up into the air. I feel as if Craig and I are being watched. Craig feels this too. A man and a woman in a boat. We watch ourselves being watched. He says, "All these guys are out here to get away from their wives."

One of Craig's newspaper colleagues asked him once, in a voice that pleaded with Craig to come clean, to tell the truth, to join the club, "Do you really enjoy fishing with your wife?" Every time Craig remembers this he laughs. He repeats it sometimes when we are making love in the tall grass beside a trout stream, or when we are stretched out naked together under the covers in our van. He leans over now and asks, smiling, "Do you really think I can have any fun fishing with my wife?"

We are dressed in heavy wool pants and sweaters and big felt-lined boots. Craig asks me, when I am dressed like this, if I think anyone can tell I am a woman. The sweater and down jacket hide my breasts. My long blonde hair is under a hat, my face is buried in wool, no one can see my earrings. What would be the thing that would make them know I was not a man among men? What is the line I would have to cross for them to know for sure that I was different from them?

"Only when I speak," I say. "Or maybe when you lean over in the boat and kiss me. Then maybe they would think I was a woman. But I wouldn't necessarily have to be."

Until recently it never occurred to me to wonder why I was the only woman I knew who walked in the woods with a shotgun looking for grouse, or sat in a duck blind or a goose blind, or crouched up in a tree with a rifle waiting for deer, or went fishing on the Rainy River. It never occurred to me to wonder because I never felt alone, before now.

I used to hate being a woman. When I was very young, I believed I was a boy. I raced boxcars made from orange crates, played football with the neighbor boys and let them experiment with my body, the parts of which seemed uninteresting to me and not valuable. I was with them, watching myself in the light in their eyes, looking at me. I was flattered in high school when someone said to me, "I like you. You're just like a guy." The words I liked best to hear were: rangy, tough, smart, cynical. My father made jokes about women's libbers burning bras. I laughed too. Throughout college I never knew what it was like to touch a woman, to kiss a woman, to have a woman as a friend. All my friends were men. I am thirty years old now, and I feel alone. I am not a man. Knowing this is like an earthquake. Just now all the lies are starting to unfold. I don't blend in as well or as easily as I used to. I refuse to stay on either side of the line.

In the boat next to ours is a quiet man with a fixed smile who has been catching all the fish. He is over a drop-off, his jig sinking exactly twenty-one feet. That is where the fish are. I ask him where he is from, my voice echoing across the water. He says he is from Warren, Minnesota. I ask him if he knows the boy I read about in the newspaper who got kicked out of West Point and was suing for his right to go back. The boy was his town's pride: a track star, a member of the choir, an honor student, handsome, full of promise. At West Point, too, he was full of promise. With his beautiful voice, he sang solo at the White House for the President. Then, on a tip from one of the boy's high school chums, the military started digging around in his past. Before they found out what he knew they would, he came forward and told them the truth. "I'm gay, sir," he told his commanding officer.

The man from Warren pushes his baseball cap back on his head and squints at the sun. He says to me, across the water, "I knew that boy really well. He was a model for the community. A model for all the younger kids." He is shaking his head. "It's hard to figure out," he says. "Just so darned hard to figure out why he'd go and do such a thing and ruin his future like that."

"I hope he wins his case against West Point," I say. There is more I ache to add. I want to yell across to him, "What's to figure out? He loves men." But I say no more and turn away, ashamed of my silence. As I turn away, the man from Warren is still shaking his head. "It's just so hard to figure out."

Craig and I came to the Rainy partly to meet and fish with some old friends of mine, Kevin and Brad, whom I met while reporting for the *Grand Forks Herald* in North Dakota. Kevin and Brad have brought their friend John with them. John is the fishing columnist for the paper and also a professor of English. He is originally from Mississippi.

Around the campfire at night, Kevin tells us about his latest assignment. He is organizing a special section on wolves. The people of Roseau, Minnesota, believe they have a wolf problem and want the Minnesota Department of Natural Resources to get rid of some of the animals.

John is slouched by the fire with his feet straight out, taking long drinks from a bottle of root beer schnapps. Brad and Craig are standing, their hands in their pockets, looking down at the flames and coals. Kevin puts a wad of chewing tobacco behind his lower lip. I squat by the fire, hunched over a mug of tea. John passes me the bottle of schnapps and I hesitate, but I am so curious to taste it. I take a small sip and make a face.

Kevin says, "Farmers think the wolf pack is purposely underestimated."

Craig asks, "You mean the government is lying about how many wolves there are so the farmers don't get upset?"

"It's more than the wolf they want to kill," I say. "It's what the wolf represents."

"What's that?" Brad says.

"Lust," I say. They laugh.

"They want control," Craig says. "They want control over nature. That's what management is all about. It's for us, not the animals. Just like with this river." Craig waves his hand toward the dark water.

"It stinks," Brad says.

"Literally," Kevin says.

"Buffalo shit," John says.

We all look at him and wait.

"Do ya'll know how much the rivers were polluted by buffalo shit? Millions of buffalo shitting in the rivers back before the white man came and after?" He's not laughing.

"Why, our screwing up the earth and killing animals, it's as natural as buffalo shit," he says. "We're part of nature too, hell. If you fuck around with nature—try to clean up the river, protect the wolves—you'll upset the whole balance of time and evolution. Just leave things be."

There is a long, uncomfortable silence. Then Craig says, "The world has had millions of years to get used to buffalo shit. But no matter how much buffalo dung there is in a river, it still will never be as bad as dioxin."

The next day, Sunday, is the day we leave. Craig and I fish from early morning until noon. When it comes time to load the boat and return to St. Paul, one of us has to get out onshore and drive the car to the boat landing. And one of us has to take the boat by water. I want to go by water, to go fast and have the spray fly up around me and the front of the boat rise out of the river.

Craig says, "You take the boat." This is what I want to do, but I am afraid.

"Really?" I ask him. "Really, I can drive it down?" I expect not to be trusted.

"What about rocks?" I ask.

"Watch out for them," he says, very casually. He has no second thoughts. He does not understand my timidity.

Once, in the spring, a friend and I sat on the steps of Lind Hall at the University of Minnesota and watched a group of boys playing on their skateboards, jumping high in the air, knees pulled up, big, orange high-tops hovering off the ground, their skateboards flipping under them, over and over. Then the boys would land safely. Then, there they would go again, taking a running leap onto a cement bench, turning on top of it and coming off again, graceful and noisy. My friend said, "Guys are brought up to think they can do everything."

I think of this as I pull away from the shore, waving at Craig. I think of my brothers, Austin and Edward, who climb cliffs and fly airplanes. Many women, I think, grow up believing they can't do anything. One of the tasks I believe I never will be able to do is backing the trailer into the water to load or launch the boat. I have tried and nearly every time have ruined something: cranked the trailer around to dangerous angles, smashed a taillight, backed off the edge of the boat ramp, put the van in reverse instead of forward and driven it into the water to the top of the wheelwells. I know that I can learn to do this physical, mechanical task. What I regret is that I do not simply *assume* I can do it. I wish I could charge into it without reserve, full of confidence, free of doubt. Like a man might.

I have learned from Craig that it is not only my gender that dictates my insecurity. When we put the boat in at the Rainy River, Craig is always nervous. He believes he is being watched and judged. But, unlike me, he is protected from ridicule. When we bought the van it came with a bumper sticker, left there by its previous owner. It says "Vietnam Veterans of America." Craig believes this sticker gives him certain privileges and encourages respect in parking lots and at boat ramps. It prevents laughter. I often think he wishes he had earned this bumper sticker rather than bought it. He was training to be a Navy pilot when the war ended and he was sent home. Sometimes when he meets a man his age and picks up a hint or a clue, he asks them, shyly, "Were you in Nam?" Sometimes they say yes and ask him if he was, and he says, almost apologetically, "No. Almost."

I drive the boat down the river, watching out for rocks. I must not hit any rocks. If I hit rocks, I will have failed. I see rocks ahead, but also a spot that looks deep. I go for what I think is the deepest water. Spray comes over the bow and sides. I am bobbing along, zooming, my hair flying out behind me, the shore whizzing past. I am doing it all by myself. My image of myself and my self come together here. I am perfect.

Then the propeller grinds against submerged rocks, the motor tilts forward and drags across them, gouging the prop, ripping the metal as easily as cloth. I crush my teeth against one another. Again, the motor tilts forward, the engine rises in pitch and there is a grating and a crunching. Again and again this happens. I cannot see the rocks. I cannot see one rock, I have no idea where they are. I feel defeated. I make it to shore, where men line the banks, and park, hitting one last rock. I pull up the motor to see the damage I have done: the prop is frayed, white paint long gone, twisted silver in its place.

I have fucked up. I never should have been trusted with this boat. I despise myself. It is not my place to drive a boat. It is too big a thing for me. Too dangerous, too demanding. Craig arrives at the boat landing. I start to cry. He says, "Don't cry. Don't cry. We needed a new prop anyway." I expect him to be angry. Instead, Craig says, "You need to learn to do this. We should have you practice. You should always drive the boat and back up the trailer, light the stove and the lantern."

I always expect anger and sometimes feel cheated and lost when I don't get it. I expect anger now, with Craig, because that is what I learned to expect from my father. That is the way my father would have reacted if I had failed in this way in front of him.

I learned many early lessons from my father and have carried them with me into womanhood. For my father there is no middle ground between success and complete failure. I learned from him to expect and strive for perfection and to truly trust no one but myself. "If you want it done right, do it yourself," he says. For my scientist father the world of nature, the world of personal relations and desire, the world of chance and fate, resembles a machine of sorts. Oil it, clean it, take care of it and it will run for you; you can prevent any problem from occurring. As long as you know a thing thoroughly, as long as you have control over it, as long as you command it, it can never surprise you. All of this I learned as a child, each lesson hardening into a code I would adhere to, mostly unwittingly, much of my adult life. Craig is not like my father. Instead of anger from him I get the opposite—laughter!

It has become tradition with us that while Craig puts the cover on the boat, tucks the life jackets away and winds up the stringer, I clean the fish. I take our collection of walleyes to the fish house and see that inside the screen door five men are working, slicing open the walleyes with long fillet knives, talking about their fishing day. "Is there room for another person in there?" I ask. I ask this because they are watching me stand outside the door, stringer in hand, wondering with their eyes what I am doing here. I feel unnatural and self-conscious. Perhaps they think of their own wives, or kids, at home and wonder why I am not there, too. One man, the oldest, the one with gray hair and pink ears, says, "It's kind of cozy in here." I say that I'll wait. I am waiting, watching them slice through the fish, peeling off an entire side of the body, then slipping the knife between the skin and the white flesh, separating the two with one or two strokes. It is remarkable to me how easy it is to slice apart a walleye—carving a breathing thing down to two essential fillets that bear no resemblance to the fish alive. The only way for me to do this is to ignore that what I've got is a fish, something that hours ago was swimming, alive.

From behind me comes a man with a stringer of fish he can barely hold up. He barrels around me, steps into the fish house and throws his fish on the counter. He is in. I am still outside.

I pick up my fish and march away. Craig sees me.

"Wouldn't they let you in?"

I say, "There's no room for a goddamned girl in that fish house."

I throw down the stringer, the knife, the cutting board, the jug of water, the plastic bags and my orange cleaning tub, fall to my knees on the ground and start slashing at my fish. One, two, three. One, two, three. Three strokes and the fillet comes off clean and smooth. I am angry. I am saying to myself, "I can do this better than any of those bastards. Better than any of them." I feel defiant and confident, proud and suddenly cruel. When I do this, I realize, I am leaping across a line between the fish's life and mine, across a line that divides life from death. And I can do it as well as any. I can move as easily as anyone across this space.

Craig wants to take a new route home. I would never dare. I would simply take the freeway, the safe and easy route. He chooses a curving line that runs through the Nett Lake Indian Reservation. We wind, bump and take twice as long, but Craig likes these roads where you cannot see where you are going. There is one right angle after another.

I am exhausted and sad. "I should give up and stay home," I say. "The worse it gets the more I see I don't have a place out here." I am looking out the window at the forest bumping past, thinking of the river, the outhouse, the fish house.

Around a sharp corner, a white and brown blur rises from the middle of the road. We see a hawk with a mouse in its claws, a wisp of a tail, four tiny feet hanging down, a little package being carried head forward into the sky by a graceful flapping bird that goes up and up and up and over the tops of the pines. Craig slows down and we both duck our heads and peer out the windows so that we can watch the hawk until it disappears.

Craig sees that I am crying. He asks me, "What are you afraid of?"

"I am tired and afraid of being the only woman. I am so lonely," I say. He is quiet.

"I'm afraid of the killing," I say. "I'm afraid that I wouldn't know how to live and not murder." I wipe my nose with the sleeve of my sweater. "The line is so thin," I say. "I'm afraid there is no difference between me and them."

Craig is quiet again for a long time and then says to me, "You know, if you don't take your place, then you'll lose it."

"I'm not sure I want it," I say. "Not here. Not like this. Not this place." In truth, *I am not sure*. Not sure at all. But there has to be a space for me; space for me as a woman out here. There has to be a middle ground. A space between the borderlines.

GROUSE

SOMETIMES WHEN WE ARE WALKING in the fall woods hunting for ruffed grouse, I hear from deep in the forest an unmistakable beating. It comes softly and rises, at the same time that it deepens and fades. It comes from everywhere and nowhere. Far away and close by. It is a sound without a beginning or an ending. Every time I hear it, the sound of grouse wings drumming the air, I think at first that it is the beating of my own heart, that the sound has risen from inside of me.

Somewhere there is a grouse, perched on a mound in the woods, or on a drumming log. The grouse is spreading its wings and beating the air, a rhythmic *thump-thump-thump* that gets louder and faster before it disappears like a ghost. Craig said at first that it was like the way an old diesel tractor starts, *thump-thump-thump-thumpthumpthumpthump*. But I don't think of tractors. Every time I hear this sound I stop, afraid that I might be dying, afraid that it is my own heart, beating itself against my breastbone, desperate in its red-ribbed cage.

On the fall roads that we walk hunting for grouse, everything is rotting and reeking, reeking sweetly. We walk for thirty seconds and then pause for thirty more. I count under my breath, "One, one-thousand . . ." as I step carefully over dense clover, keeping an eye out for Craig who is walking parallel to me in the thick forest brush. When we stop, we listen carefully for the sound of grouse walking in the leaves. We listen for faint scratchings and grouse voices. We look for movement.

I pick up leaves and put them in my pockets. I pick up yellow leaves, already dry, and I think of things that have nothing to do with hunting. I think of papyrus—the paper the ancient Egyptians made from the tall sedge that grew in the Nile Valley. I think of how the Egyptians must have written on such beautiful paper while lounging in barges on the Nile.

I think of the Egyptian men standing thin and two-dimensional, with red legs, chests, arms and faces, and long black hair that is strandless, like helmets. I think of Cleopatra sending love letters to Mark Antony and letters of hate to Caesar on paper like this dried leaf; letters written in purple ink with the tip of a peacock feather.

Up ahead I see a grouse that has stopped by the side of the road to fill its crop with clover and gravel. It is an easy shot. I brace myself, legs apart, boots planted firmly on the road, raise my shotgun, take aim and pull the trigger. When I get to it, my ears still ringing, the grouse is dead. Some of its feathers are spread around on the colored leaves, and its blood has marked this spot. I put the feathery, warm bundle into the back pocket of my canvas hunting vest and keep walking.

I walk for thirty seconds and I wait for thirty more. As I walk I pick up more leaves. This time a maple leaf that is yellow and speckled with red. And the perfect, warm, brown leaf of an oak. I think of the veins in my mother's hands, like the veins in this leaf, except hers are blue and pink; blue and pink and covered with white dish soap or bread dough, her wedding band almost hidden by swelling.

Craig and I take the grouse we have each gotten back to our car. While we are skinning them Craig tells me the story of a man with whom he once hunted, who when he shot a grouse would put it down on the ground, put a boot over each wing and then with one swift motion, rip the breast right off the bird, leaving the carcass there on the forest floor.

Craig takes the liver from the grouse he shot and he walks way back into the woods and places the small dark red of it in the crook of two branches of a red maple. "It's silly," he says to me, coming back, wiping his bloody hands on his jeans. He is asking me if putting the liver in the tree is all right, asking me to reassure him this is a good thing to do. "No, it's not silly," I say. "It's a good, serious thing."

WOLF

I AM DEER HUNTING, twenty feet up in an icy popple tree that is covered with frozen rain. My hands ache. The wind burns my face. I feel the unmasked skin around my eyes pucker and crack. All my senses are alert for movement in the woods. A leaf sails down to the ground, startling me. A woodpecker lands on a branch within my reach and pokes at a tree limb, *rat-tat-tat*. The sound echoes in the frozen air. Farther away, four fat gray and brown grouse fly into another popple tree and walk their way like penguins to the top branch.

Craig and I walked here early in the darkness, in the black-gray light just before dawn, not using flashlights, but letting our eyes get accustomed to the dimness as we moved slowly, heating up fast in our heavy clothes, lifting our knees high in the snow. I climbed this tree, hand over hand, hoisting myself, with my rifle and my backpack, up onto this safe, sturdy limb. For a while, all I heard was my labored breathing. But then everything became silent. And the cold started taking away my heat, my breath, and ice crystals began to form on the outside of my scarf.

I am waiting now for a deer in this silence and fighting darkness; fighting the anxious terror that comes from inside of me, like hands groping, whenever I am not occupied with an immediate task, whenever I am waiting; fighting the darkness that comes whenever I am still and whenever I allow myself to think about my sister Ally, who died when she was twenty-two, who killed herself by taking an overdose of anti-depressants. Twenty feet above the earth, suspended, looking out over the red brush, golden grass and yellow tamaracks of a northern Minnesota woods, in this quiet, I am pulled into darkness.

She hears noise like wind blowing. She hears no one talking. She hears silence surrounding Ally's death. Her father, her mother, her brothers, not talking, not talking about Ally. "No use in opening old wounds," her mother says. "No use in grieving." She sees colors, mostly yellow, behind her eyes. She sees that everything in her life now has something to do with Ally's death. If someone asked her now, "Do you love anyone?" she would say, "Yes, Ally." She feels as if she is floating. She wants to crawl into the grave with her sister. Darkness fights with light. Darkness fights with clear, sharp pain. She pushes the darkness away, shakes her head. It comes on anyway.

What Ally did wrong was try to tell the truth; the truth about their family. And in this one way, she was fearless, wide open. Ally couldn't lie anymore, wouldn't be quiet. "We're not a regular family," Ally said. "Can't you see?" Ally tried to make her hear, wanted her to see, but then, like the others, she didn't listen to her sister. "You're forgetting everything," she told Ally. "What about the hikes up Millcreek Canyon? The trips to the zoo? Hearing Mom read us Moby Dick, all gathered up around her on the couch? Be thankful," she told Ally. "You love to make trouble, don't you?" She thought then that her sister was only angry, maybe crazy, that what she needed was three months alone in the woods, a course in mountain climbing, something to shake her up, make her believe in herself. She thought then that her sister was imagining things. Ally wrote her letters: "Face it, Gretchen," she said, "mother is an alcoholic." She wrote back: "You can't say that. You can't say that about your mother." Ally wrote her more letters: "Forget it, Gretchen, there's no hope for me and our father. He'll never listen." She wrote back: "Why do you fight with him? You only make it worse."

She starts to cry. She thinks, Ally knew we are all fucked up. What she knows now, what she sees and understands, what Ally tried to tell her, sits like a stone in her chest. In this vicious grayness she thinks she sees answers. Rule number one: You must pay attention. You cannot ignore

anything, or someone will die. She sees her life every day as a terrible
struggling against forces that drown out peace and smother light. Forces
that make things fall apart. Her center holds not by miracle or luck, but
by sheer force of will. She thinks, I will not go mad.

This blackness is always inches away from her heels and her back.
Anything, any slip, and it can swallow her. Constant vigilance is neces-
sary. Pushing forward is necessary. If she lets it pull her backward she will
fall, dark earth closing up around her and her falling, pulled down and
down by darkness, looking around, confused, her hair like tangled tree
roots curving around her face, filling her mouth, her eyes, her ears.

She pulls up from this dream, wherever she is, in a duck blind, in a fish-
ing boat, or in a tall popple waiting for deer, by imagining herself rising
up out of the earth, springing forth, gasping, with rivulets of dirt coming
off her, exploding from some subterranean depth, dirt clods flying. She
springs up in bed, twisted with sheets and wet with sweat, yelling, "Ally!
Ally!"

In front of me, the sun has begun to rise, spreading orange light over everything in the woods, and I pull the visor of my parka hood down to
shade my eyes. I am back into some light, back into what seems to me
more real; me sitting in a popple tree that is slick with frozen rain.

Behind me and to my right I see grayness moving. All the animals
except some birds are shades of gray or brown in the woods. Easier not
to be seen. I think I am seeing a fawn with spots, which is unlikely in
November, but not impossible. The gray shape glides through the willow and brown grass. A long nose. Two dark eyes. A thick neck. A
straight back.

A coyote.

Or a wolf.

It trots below me, paws lanky and loose, making noise in the grass.
Swish. Swish. Leaves collapse under its wide feet. It has no idea I am
above it looking down. I want to make it acknowledge me. I want to say,
"Hey, wolf!" But I wait. I am quiet and amazed. I want to see how it would
be if I were not here. I imagine myself here and not here, seeing but not
watching.

The wolf heads out into the open grassland between the popples and the woods. It stops beneath me. I could jump down on it, drop my orange glove on its yellow-gray back. I want it to know I am here. I want to see its wolf eyes. It stops and turns around and goes back into the woods, gracefully, as it came.

When I see Craig at noon I tell him about the wolf. He has been sitting across a clearing from me in a tall tree. I keep track of him by looking for his orange parka. When he climbs down I do too, and we meet on the logging road near his tree. "I saw a wolf or a coyote," I say.

Craig takes me gently by the shoulders, a bunch of the fabric of my hunting parka in each mitten. "You saw a wolf?" he repeats.

"Or a coyote."

"Either way, you're lucky," he says. "Either way." For both of us, to see any animal in the woods—a chickadee, a black moose, a deer, even to hear a mouse scurrying beneath dry leaves—is to join with some part of a wilder world.

"It had a long tail," I say, stretching out my arms. "I'm sure it was a wolf."

"How big?" he asks.

"This tall," I say, my hand at my waist.

"It was a wolf," he says. We walk out of the woods, feeling humbled and uplifted. It is a gift to see a wolf. We walk in the rain to the van where we will have some soup and coffee and take a nap.

When we get to the van and are taking off our mittens and coats and unloading our guns, another hunter drives up in a black pickup truck. While his wife waits in the truck, the man in the orange sweatshirt with a cigarette dangling from his lip, his hands in the pockets of his bluejeans, comes over to talk to us. "Get anything?"

I had. A small buck. I had killed it and cleaned it and put a piece of its liver on the highest branch of a bush. For a hawk. Or a goddess.

"I see you did." He eyeballs the deer on the ground by our car.

"It's small," I say. It is small. Tiny, really. Its horns are only as big as nipples. We feel lucky. Even this tiny deer will give us meat to eat for most of the winter and its hide will cover our feet in soft slippers.

"It'll be good to eat," he says.

"We saw a wolf," Craig says. He is smiling, excited.

"Those timberwolves," the man says. "There're two packs here now, a pack of eight and a pack of ten. They really cut into the deer herd." The man shakes his head. "I live right by here." He points to the north. "Christ, you hear 'em howl at night. It sends shivers up my back." He shivers. "I haven't seen a deer all day."

"Yeah," we say. We don't want to tell him we have seen plenty of deer besides the one I shot. We saw four, their tall white tails zig-zagging through the brush. And in the quiet tamarack I saw a horse-sized buck which, before I could get my rifle off my shoulder and untangled from my parka hood string, got up in slow motion and bounded away.

"They oughta just pack those wolves up and send 'em to Washington," he says, "where they belong."

Some noise fills her head. There is a voice saying, "Be quiet." She wants to say to this man in her most vulgar language, "Fuck you, asshole. You're the one we should pack up and send away." There is a lot of noise in her brain. A lot of violence going on. It feels to her like water just let go from a dam crashing through a small culvert. It is a whooshing. A pressure. She loses her sense of place and time. She rises above herself in her blaze-orange jacket and above this man and Craig, above the woods where she can see wolves and deer in the trees and brush. Along with the voice that says "Quiet" there is another voice and to her it sounds like Ally's, soft and insistent now: "You can't ignore this. You must speak to this ignorance. You must speak to this cruelty. You must say something. Say something." She thinks she owes her this. She owes it to Ally to learn this lesson. If it is all she can do for her now, she will learn this lesson. She will learn to speak. She will learn to say something real. But she can't talk. Her words are frozen. She thinks if she said what is in her heart something terrible would happen. Something would break or snap, in her, in this man she so wants to speak to. Someone would get angry.

The man leaves, spinning the wheels of his truck on the frozen ground. I ask Craig if we should have said something.

"I didn't want to tell him about all the deer," he says. Neither did I.

Because then the next morning the man would be in our spot, maybe in my tree.

"But about the wolves," I say.

"Right," Craig says. "They aren't our deer. On the other hand, what is a wolf? It could be about economics. If you live out here and try to get a living from the land and a wolf is eating your cattle, it's hard to think about natural order."

"That's not what we're talking about. Cattle, I mean. He lives in the city, that man," I say.

"You're right," Craig says.

I vow that the next time someone talks to me about wolves, or any animal, in the same way as the man in the orange sweatshirt, I will say something. Anything. "They aren't our deer," I will say. "They are the wolves' deer first."

At the end of the weekend, Craig and I drive to meet his aunt Bea and her husband Bob in Roseau, Minnesota. They are headed to St. George, Utah for the winter. We want to say goodbye and have some dinner. Craig turns on the heat and we speed along while the heavy smell of wet wool fills our van.

Bob reminds me of my father and of my grandfather too. He is German, knows the value of a dollar, lines up his wrenches in order of size on the wall behind his workbench. He has gray hair and a thin gray mustache, like my grandfather, Frederick Wilhelm Legler, and like my father too. But he is also unlike these men I know. My favorite picture of Bob is a snapshot of him squeezed into a tiny go-cart, a red Shriner's fez tilting on his head, waving at the camera. This ignoble frivolity is something my father, and his father, would never stoop to. Because of this, I have liked Bob and I have trusted him.

We settle in around a table at the Holiday Inn. "Let us pray," Bob says, and reaches out his hand for mine. I reach out mine for Craig's and he does the same to his aunt. We form a circle and Bob and Bea bow their heads and close their eyes. I never pray like this. I watch everyone else while they close their eyes and move their lips and I wonder what they are really thinking. I have never believed in this kind of god. "For all of this we are truly grateful, Amen," Bob says, and we clink our cocktail glasses together.

Craig and Bob start talking about football. Craig does not watch football, but this is something he can talk about with Bob.

"Gee, how about those Vikings?" Craig says.

"How did that Walker boy do?" Bob asks.

Bea's eyes go back and forth between the men as if she is watching a ping-pong ball bounce between two players. She breaks in. "Can I interrupt this conversation?" She thinks this is what women are supposed to do: keep men civilized, keep them from talking about football.

"O.K.," Craig says.

"How are the girls?" She means Craig's daughters, who live with their mother, Craig's first wife, in Taylors Falls, Minnesota.

"Fine," he says. This is the end of their conversation. Craig is irritated with his aunt for breaking in.

Then I tell Bob, "We saw a wolf." There is a pause and I am smiling, waiting for him to tell me how wonderful this is, how lucky I am to have met one of these elusive beings, one of these mysterious creatures.

"I've seen timberwolves while up in a deer stand," he says. I am smiling, waiting to compare stories with him about their beauty. My heart is wide open.

"But I could never get a bead on 'em," he says. "Never was lucky enough to kill one from a deer stand."

My food is dry in my mouth.

"But I got one in Canada once," he says. "Bea won't let me spread it out on the living-room floor. She thinks it doesn't go with the carpet or the couch." He laughs and winks at Bea and she rolls her eyes.

I remember the wolf skin now, rolled up and stuck among boxes of Christmas ornaments and gardening trowels. When I'd gone into the basement the summer before to clean walleyes in the sink in the laundry I had seen it there, and I had pulled it out of the box, stroked the yellow-gray fur. I had laughed. It was ludicrous, really. The big yellow glass eyes, the pathetic pale-pink plastic tongue and the sinister snarling lips curling back over plastic fangs.

"So, you killed that one?" I ask, my voice steady and cold. I had imagined somehow that he had got it at a garage sale, or that it had been given to him by a friend.

He tells us he was fishing in the winter and everyone was shooting the wolves. I want to know the whole story.

"Everyone?" I ask.

He says, "In the late afternoon the wolves would come out onto the ice of the lake and cavort, you know, jump around and chase each other. Man, it was some sight to see, those wolves, some gray and some black, just playing like that." Bob makes a dancing motion with his arms and shoulders. "So, I just went out one evening and I got me one between the lake and the shore and I shot it." Bob holds up his arms as if he is holding a rifle and says, "*Wham!*"

I ask if it was legal then, whenever it was, to shoot wolves, because, you know, I say, they're an endangered species now. He laughs. "I don't care," he says. "That's rubbish. Everyone was doing it."

Her face fades, her smile melting away like hot wax. Her body curls up around her heart. She is shrinking. She is looking through the scope of a rifle, the thin crosshairs centered on a wolf. She hears a crack, sees the wolf's body fall in a spasm into the grass and just as it goes down it turns its clear yellow eyes to her and she shudders. In those eyes she sees some kind of misery, some kind of knowledge of betrayal, and she feels a nauseating guilt fill her up. If she could only speak, she thinks, if only she had spoken, if only she had listened, it would have all been different. She rises up again in her gray wool pants and boots and hovers over this dinner table. She sees four people trying to engage clumsily and fiercely in some kind of love. She sees a woman among these four who is glowing red with fear and anger. She starts to remember things. Images go past as if on a speeding filmstrip. Sounds blur together in one long moan. She is reading Ally's journal from the week before her sister died. "I can't talk to anyone," Ally wrote. "I try to talk to Eddie, but he doesn't understand, and I can't talk to Gretty either. They see death differently than I do." She is letting her anger pulse through her veins like acid. October 1984: Ally wrote that she couldn't work and go to school and take her medication too. The pills set her heart skittering, beating wildly. She had to spend hours every day at the gym to counter the side-effects. She went to their mother and father for money. "He told me he wouldn't pay for school unless I went full-time. 'There are certain responsibilities you must take on as an

adult,' he said," Ally wrote. "*I went to them for help and I felt betrayed.*"
*Christmas 1984: Ally wrote that she took their mother's glass and poured
the white wine in it down the kitchen sink. She didn't know what else to
do, she said, to get her to stop drinking.*

*The noise in her head is getting louder. Things are spinning. There is
chaos in her head. Someone is holding her back and someone is pushing
her forward. "Quiet," one voice says. This is my voice. "Say something,"
the other voice says. This is Ally's voice. Everything is thin now, and dangerous. She is entering dangerous territory. Something is ready to shatter.
She knows she could blow up this tenuous gathering. Her words could be
like dynamite. She already has wounded everyone at this table, so fragile
is the crust of their relationship. She wants to explain something to Bob,
to have it make sense. She wants to speak. Why kill such a beautiful
animal for nothing, she wants to ask him. Not to eat, not to feed your body,
but to take its skin and fold it into a box in a dank basement? Why hate
a wolf for eating a deer? Why murder a wolf for trying to live the only way
it knows how?*

"The wolves and the deer are all God's creatures," I say, my voice urgent
and shaking, trying to speak to Bob in a way I think he will understand.
"Na," he shakes his head. Craig is watching me nervously.
"They're not our deer," I say, my voice more firm. "They're not *your* deer."

*The more she talks the less the pressure, the softer the noise, the closer she
gets to light. She feels as if she is swimming up through dark earth towards
sun rays on the surface, her hair flowing down her back in thick strands,
her legs kicking, her hands pushing and pulling the earth around her in
muddy swirls.*

"They're not *our* deer," I say again. I lay my fork on the table.
"The wolves have ruined mucho hunting spots for me," he says.
"We can go to the grocery store. The wolves can't," I say.
Hunting is a privilege for me, not a right, not a necessity. I choose it. I

will not starve if I don't shoot a deer one fall. I have no claim to the deer in the woods, even to the tiny buck I shot this year. When I hunt I am a stranger, a visitor, leaving my circle and entering another, entering the circle of wolves and deer, where I have a duty to walk quietly and respectfully, as much as I can, honoring them both. I would not shoot a wolf to save a deer for myself. I want Bob to know all of this, to understand.

"They're a plague. Best thing to do is get rid of them," Bob says of the wolves.

Words are collecting within her. The voice of Ally is in her, and the face of the wolf. They say, together, "You must speak to this." Ally tried to tell a truth and no one listened. "Look, look at how it is all wrong," she wrote. "It's not my fault," she wrote. "It's not my fault that I'm so crazy. Look around you, what we grew up with." Ally spoke into dark clouds, into thick mist. No one heard her, or if they heard they twisted her words. They preferred silence to her truth. No more silence. She owes it to Ally, she thinks, to learn this lesson, to do this one thing. To speak and then to live.

A voice is growing in her. The voice rises from her belly into her throat and when it comes out it sounds to her like a long, ragged howl. It feels to her like her guts are being ripped from within her. "Wrong," she says. "Wroooong."

I am out of any darkness now and I am not floating. The backs of my legs feel the hard seat of my chair. What I say does not sound like a howl to Craig and Bob and Bea. I say, looking at the steak on my plate, the half-eaten vegetables, "It's funny why a deer is worth killing and saving to eat and a wolf is worth killing for nothing, not meat, not anything but meanness." I look at Bob, straight in the eye, and say again, "Not anything but meanness."

GOOSEBERRY MARSH,
PART ONE

A T GOOSEBERRY MARSH our canoe splits through thin ice. Craig and I push the silver bow against the frozen bank, and I gather up our ducks: ducks whose bodies I scooped from the water after they had fallen from the autumn sky, whose necks I wrung one by one, whose blood is on my hands.

Onshore I slit their bellies with my pocketknife and reach two fingers into the sticky, velvet, still-hot caves, pulling out livers, lungs, the long cords the ducks speak through, and the hearts.

Gooseberry Marsh is a made-up name, pulled out of the air because the words felt full on our tongues. Swamp grass rings it. Goose nests on man-made pillars ring it. Sky rings it.

This year is a dry year, and going out at dawn, we had to pull our canoe over the shallow places between the two big ponds. The murky gas of rotting and growing things rose up from the craters our boots make in the mud. The mud, as deep as I am tall, wanted to pull me down, like hands to a bed.

After I have gutted them, I gather up our ducks in two hands and take them up the hill to the car. They swing by their soft orange feet against my thighs. Their bodies are still heavy. I line them up on the grass: three mallards, one small green teal, four bluebills, their beaks pointing toward the cattails where we hid, waiting for them to cup their wings and sail down into our decoys. I close each of their tiny eyes. In front of each mouth I dribble a miniscule mountain of yellow cornmeal, from a box with a blue Quaker smiling. And then I grab handfuls of cornmeal and throw them—to the east, to the west, to the north, to the south, and where I am right now, the place I am standing with dead ducks at my feet.

What should be said?

I don't speak, but each time the grains of cornmeal fly out and hang for a moment in the air, then fall, I think of how we will eat these ducks—roast them quickly in a hot oven with only pepper and salt on the breasts, or roast them for hours in a big pan with raisins and apples. I think of how they will taste, how the kitchen will smell, and how, when we eat, someone will roll one of the pellets that killed these birds around and around on their tongue.

Snow starts to fall on the marsh, the flakes taken up into the pond, dissolving, like wafers. The sky is the color of steel. I have saved the eight hearts. When Craig comes up from the canoe with the last load—a camouflage tarp and a bag of decoys—I give him half of the hearts and we walk down to the water, the hearts small and soft in our palms, like beads of dough, and we throw them back to the sky, calling out loud, *fly!*

Before the hearts fall into the amber water, I see wings unfold, and mallards and teal and bluebills rising up.

WILDFLOWERS

M Y MOTHER IS MOVING around the trailer, putting the crust on a blueberry pie. My father, who is tying flies at the back table, needs a pheasant neck from the closet and wants to move by my mother in the tiny space between the table and the sink. He sighs.

She is fragile; her shoulder bones, under baggy sweatshirts, poke into my breasts when I embrace her. Her face and eyes are fading, her auburn hair is filling up with gray. He too looks breakable, his skin sinking closer to his bones. They are both smaller now than I ever remember them. Even so, they crowd each other. My mother flattens herself against the sink and my father tries to get by without touching her. She winks at me. "I guess there's just no room here for me anymore," she says.

We are in Yellowstone National Park on a family vacation, only no one is here but me, Craig, and my parents. My brothers Edward and Austin couldn't come. But we still do this vacation because it is something sure. We hang onto it tenaciously. Someone always goes to Yellowstone every fall.

This is the Yellowstone that burned in 1988, the biggest fire ever in a national park. Craig was at the fire taking pictures for the *St. Paul Pioneer Press and Dispatch*. He shows me around, positive and powerful, his black camera swinging over his shoulder, his chest solid in a plaid shirt, his feet wrapped in the security of leather boots, his head capped by a gray Stetson.

"See that?" he says, pointing to a hillside. "This was solid black, this hillside. Burned down to the soil. Black. The only color here was black. Solid. All the way up that hill." He squats and digs in the dirt with his finger. "The grasses came back. See how strong they are?" At the meadow between the villages of Norris and Mammoth he says, "This was all blackened too. Smoking. Every day you'd come through here and choke." Now there is purple fireweed all over and green grass.

The fireweed has covered whole areas of burn in a sea of lavender. Mixed with the color is the smell of burn, a sodden, sweet and sour after-fire smell of watery ash. It is the smell of Craig's skin after we make love. In other spots the forest floor is still recovering from fire that burned straight down to and through the soil. Bark peels off the trees like blackened chicken skin, but at the base of the tree green shoots are already coming up. A big strong lodgepole is reduced to a standing pillar of charcoal that flakes off at the touch. I break loose a piece of charcoal and draw with it. I draw the shapes of purple asters, white yarrow, daisies, bright red Indian paintbrush and goldenrod. I draw tall black bars of burned lodgepole pines, their branches naked and shining silver in the sun.

Early in the morning Craig and I and my father hike to the meadow to fish. We sit on the same gray log we always do, take off our hiking boots, pull on wading shoes, and head off along the stream, our feet crunching in the watery gravel. The stream makes its way through the meadow like music, fast and slow, muddy and clear, around sandy bars, through deep pools and past undercut banks from which grasshoppers leap. The sky here is mercurial. In the morning it is a wash of lavender and pink, the colors of a soft blanket. In the noon heat the sky gapes open, metallic blue. In the evening it is yellow and gold, the colors of a cutthroat trout's sleek sides.

By ten o'clock I have caught a fish, an 18-inch-long thick-bellied cutthroat, which I pick from the stream by its tail with my wet red bandana. After Craig takes my picture I unloose the tiny deer-hair grasshopper from the fish's lip and slip the fish back into the stream. I don't catch many fish anymore. It is not because I can't cast. At that I am "a natural," my father has said. I can throw out a heavy line tipped with a tiny fly and have that fly land at the opposite bank as softly as a dandelion star lands in the grass. Skill is not my problem. It is attitude. I hear my father say to Craig downstream, his voice carried to me in the thin air, "Her problem is she's too impatient. She's not persistent enough." At noon I crawl up onto the grassy bank and change, putting on dry socks and boots for the hike back to the trailer. "Why are you leaving?" my father calls to me across the water.

I say, "To go be with mom."

"Why?"

I yell, "To talk. And look for flowers. And make a pie."

There are so many wildflowers this year. My mother wants to look close to the trailer because she can't walk far. She smokes a lot. Sometimes I think she will die any minute. Then she surprises me by being funny and strong. I ask her, "When shall we eat lunch?" She says, "As soon as I *hot up* the beans." I laugh.

"Where did you get that?"

She says, "From Festus on *Bonanza*. Or was it *Gunsmoke*?"

We are naming all the flowers we find. We each have a book. We name the flowers not to own them, not to brag hollowly that we know them. We don't name them to suggest that by knowing their names we know all about them. We are not naming them to catalogue them or control them, but to speak with them and each other.

My mother asks me, "Shouldn't you be fishing?"

I tell her I've become confused about fishing and don't know why I do it anymore. All I know is that right now I want to be with her. Then she asks me, "Have you become a somber person? You don't laugh much anymore." I am shocked to hear this. I didn't know it showed. "You have guilt written in your face," she says. My mother figures we have control over just a very small portion of our lives. "Accidents happen," she says. "To good people." I struggle daily with belief in the opposite—that we can control much more. That we can be commanders even of our own desires.

The flowers are growing everywhere, sprouting rebelliously in the burned-out areas amid black skeletons of sagebrush and singed earth. My mother and I are not taking this flower hunting seriously. It is a manufactured activity for us to do something together. We see a flower that is new, then open the book and try to find the picture that matches. We see birchleaf spirea from the rose family. It is shrubby with clusters of tiny white flowers. We see the common cow parsnip, an obscenely thick, green-trunked plant with white flowers on top. We see northern bedstraw, timothy, heartleaf arnica. We see cinquefoil, which my mother tells me deer eat in the winter and tastes like creosote. We see mountain snowberries. We want to find some pussytoes because they sound so nice.

My mother wants to talk about Ally.

Ally tried to kill herself more than once—with a hunting knife, a bottle of aspirin and a razor blade, finally with an overdose of anti-depressants. The pills sent her flipping and curling into massive seizures that jerked her body apart and stopped her heart and killed her brain. The doctors pumped charcoal through her body to purify her, but the poison was too strong.

"It was so awful, Gretty," my mother says. "She was lying there with the tube in her nose and charcoal all around her pretty mouth. Dad and I went in holding hands and all I could focus on was her toes. She had such big toes. I'd never noticed her toes before. They were blue. We touched her face and kissed her and I said, 'Goodbye sweetheart.'" The sounds come out of my mother's mouth in tiny, jagged bursts.

"Could I tell you something?" my mother asks me. We are still in the woods. We have found a new flower. Lupine. It is purple. "Yes," I say.

"I want to tell you something important."

"Yes."

"I didn't know about Ally's ashes," she says. "I didn't know they weren't at the mortuary. I didn't know they were in your brother's computer room, on the bookshelf." I have visions of my sister's ashes falling into the aquarium, the water instantly smoky-black, her body dissolved in water swimming with tropical fish. "Then when Austin and Mary were splitting up I told your father we should make sure about them, make sure we knew where they were. Do you know what he said to me?"

"What did he say?"

"He had tears in his eyes and he said, 'It's all taken care of.'"

Racing through my head is the idea that he took the ashes and dumped them somewhere, in a lake, in a garden, or took them up to his laboratory to keep them safe.

"He said, 'And don't ever mention it again unless I bring it up first. That's all I want to hear about it.'"

"He's always carting things off," I say.

"Calm down," my mother says. "You can't blame him. He comes from a time when men found it hard to express emotion." She continues. "After Ally died you know what he said to me? He said, 'I never really knew Ally.'"

"He never knew any of us," I say. Like many fathers he was a distant and fearful vision, leaving early, coming home late. A loud voice. A big hand. A ringing laugh. A hairy arm. Not a person. "He didn't know any of us. Not at all like you knew us," I say. "But especially he didn't know Ally."

"Well, he may not have, but I did," my mother says. "And I miss her. I miss her every day."

"Me too," I say.

"Now I just want a little place to go and put some flowers," my mother says. "It's important to have a place to go." She pauses. "It's been five years."

"I know," I say.

"Time to bury Ally's ashes," she says. "We could all grow from that."

I say, "Yes. Something good could come of it."

I want to keep looking forever, wandering in the woods with my mother. On the other hand, what I have wanted from her all these years, secretly, without knowing it fully myself, is for her to say to me, "Go on with your life. I'll be O.K. I won't die if you turn around, and even if I do, you'll go on living." But when she goes back to the trailer, I feel abandoned. I keep looking for flowers. I follow a steep trail high above Slough Creek. Topping a rise I come, breathless, upon the eye sockets of an elk skull, bleached white, stuck crookedly in the "V" of a tree. I think of William Golding's *Lord of the Flies*. I expect this skull to talk to me, to tell me truths.

My sister Ally was obsessed with death. The thread of her life and the thread of my mother's life were twisted into the same strand. "If she dies," Ally told me, "I would have to die too."

I am always afraid alone in the woods, but I push on. It starts to rain and I sit under a pine tree on a log where I get wet anyway. When I get up to go I feel silly. I don't enjoy the woods alone. There is a great space between me and anything, a flower, a fish, a pinecone, that is empty until there is another person there to share it with.

Ally is the only woman I have kissed on the lips for pure love. We slept in the same bed sometimes, arms and legs intertwined, heads resting together. We held hands in the street. I don't have that anymore. Not with anyone. Not that kind of necessary intimacy. I want my sister back. I want her back every day.

As I start back to the trailer I smell something sweet in the air blowing at me and I know it is something dead. I follow the smell to its source. Behind a huge pine lie three elk, mouths open, teeth bared, eye sockets empty. A cow and her calves perhaps. Their hides are the same color as the soil. Around them, growing in their decay, are shoots of green grass. Their skulls are partly white and partly matted with hair and tissue. Their legs are splayed, as if they suddenly collapsed. Their fuzzy hides are sunken down into caved-in, empty rib cages. Bones protrude. The fire burned off some of their range, then came a heavier snow than usual and they starved to death. All three of the elk are nose to nose.

GABIMICHIGAMI

I T IS MORNING. I wake up to a confusion of diffused yellow light sinking down on me through the bright tent dome. I am in a canoe camp Craig and I have made on a cliff at Gabimichigami. We are in the Boundary Waters Canoe Area Wilderness, three days' paddle from our car at Sea Gull Lake.

I start to dress. Craig has been up for an hour and has lit the stove. There will have to be breakfast, then dishes, then packing the canoe and paddling the canoe, then hauling the canoe over portages to another camp, then on to another, and then back to the city. I have no desire to leave; no desire to move, to go forward into the day. Reluctantly, I start pulling a blue shirt over my bare body. I start to button it, then stop.

She doesn't want clothes.

She undresses, lets the shirt fall. Her boots are set outside the tent door, laces in the dirt, damp from the water in the air. She ignores them.

She doesn't want shoes.

She wants her feet to be bare.

She does not pretend that she is dressed. She knows she is naked. But she walks outside without any shyness, with the same confidence of movement she would have if she were covered in bluejeans and a red wool jacket and her green hat.

Craig sits by the lake drinking coffee. She walks into the woods, away from him. He turns his head and sees her. She has never done this before.

35

She wonders if he will think she is strange. She wonders if he will follow her, and is glad when he does not. He says nothing.

The sky is gray and the big lake is duller and darker than the sky. In this dull light every color is accentuated, especially her skin. Her skin is white. The whiteness of her skin is like a thick, pale candle with a flame deep inside of it. In this light, the trees radiate greenness. In this light, blue veins glow through her skin.

She grabs the arm of a spruce and it springs back. She reaches for it again and puts it onto her shoulder and rubs it around there. She picks up a long pine needle from the ground and puts one end of it in her mouth. She is chewing on it. She puts her back against the thin bark of a birch tree.

Her shoulders and her hips and her thighs are softer than anything else: softer than pinecones or small chips of greenstone scattered around. She is the softest thing in the forest and the smoothest.

She is walking around trees and bushes and ducking under branches, naked. Some water is falling on her back. Her feet curve around rocks and moss and twigs. Wet leaves stick to her heels. She isn't cold. The air is still and as warm as she is. It is August.

She thinks her body is fine, out here.

Fine.

She wants to stay in the forest for a longer time.

But Craig calls to me.

"Come here and listen."

I walk to him, past the tent, where I reach in and grab shorts and my blue shirt. He is still sitting by the lake. I smell his coffee. I sit down by him on a rock. I imagine her bare skin against this rock. He says, very softly, "Listen."

I ask, "What for?"

"For nothing," he says. "There is no sound."

BEAUTIFUL LAND

HALFWAY ACROSS SOUTH DAKOTA I turned to Craig and said, "If I were a pioneer this is where I would start to panic." The hard flatness, the land rutted by dry gulches and scattered with ramshackle barns, made my heart ache. It looked as if nothing could live out there. The horizon was indistinct, just fading off into nowhere, into everywhere. I felt lost in all that space.

When we told Craig's mother in Minnesota that we were going to take her three granddaughters, Craig's kids Kim and Steff and Erikka, through South Dakota and across Wyoming to Yellowstone National Park that summer, she said "Through *that* Godforsaken wasteland?" Craig said, "No, no Ma. It's God's country."

As I stared out the passenger window of the van I asked myself what made me, like her, expect that the landscape would yield up its beauty to me easily. Remember, I said to myself, the West is complicated land. You need real sympathy for it, and patience, to get out of it what's good.

The plan for our trip was that after we spent a week with his daughters in Yellowstone, Craig would drop me off so that I could spend ten days alone with my mother and father on their new land—thirty acres in southwestern Montana, on a bluff overlooking the Madison River. I would stay ten days because I hadn't spent any time at all with my parents in years, and because that is how long it would take Craig to leave and then to come back and get me. He would drive the kids back to their mother's house in Minnesota in time for them to get ready for school. Craig would return to work for a week in St. Paul, then drive back to Montana to fetch me.

We planned then to continue across the mountains to Oregon and down the coastal highway, through the redwoods to California, then back across the plains, across Nevada, across the salt flats in Utah, back up into the humid green of a midwestern late summer, to Minnesota.

In Yellowstone I had a nightmare. We were camped with our van at Slough Creek, one of the wilder, less developed Yellowstone campgrounds, where deer walked through our camp each day as the light faded into evening, and where the sound of the water kept up a steady hiss and rumble in the night. In the creek that evening we had seen a water ouzel diving into the foaming swirls.

Well past midnight, after the girls had gone to sleep in the tent outside, after Craig and I had settled in the van, I woke and before me, stretched out above me, I saw and felt the dim forms of my own arms, my own hands, reaching up and pressing hard against the wood of the van roof, trying to make space for myself.

In the nightmare I had felt closed in, suffocated. When I awoke I was choking, my breath held in by my own closed throat. I called out to Craig in a harsh, forced whisper, "Where am I?" Then, slowly coming to realize that I was safe, that I was only imagining danger, I said again, softly, "Tell me where I am."

In the morning, I asked Craig if he would panic if he were buried alive. That's what it felt like in my nightmare. He said, "Probably." I said, "I think that would be the most awful thing, to be hemmed in like that, to have no room at all, and to know that no matter what you did, it wouldn't help. You'd yell and scream and pound on the sides and you'd just be wasting your breath in the darkness."

I had prepared Craig's daughters for my father. Craig told them, too, "He doesn't like kids." I said, "That's not it exactly. But you have to be sure and behave around him." They wanted to know why. "Is he mean?" they asked. "Sort of," I said. As soon as I said it I was embarrassed, feeling as if I were exaggerating. But I was worried for them, worried that they might be startled by his temper, or have their feelings hurt, that he might treat them as he had treated me, as he had treated my brothers and my sister, when we were young.

The way I felt as a child was nothing, I suppose, that anyone would call out of the ordinary—just a daily feeling of being afraid; afraid of having the television on too loud, afraid of asking to stop for a soda or a malt, afraid of speaking, of having desires, of wanting, afraid of doing something (anything) wrong or badly or too slowly or not enough. That's how I remember it. I didn't want Craig's daughters to be afraid. I wanted to do for them what no one had ever done for me: I wanted to protect them from his anger. But already I was telling them they had to behave, as if it (whatever it might turn out to be) was already their fault.

We left the park through West Yellowstone, that funny, touristy but still cowboyish western outpost, and kept heading west into Montana, through a valley made not long ago by the violence of an earthquake; a force that rearranged the entire landscape in minutes.

As we drove, I rolled the window down and stuck my head out into the cool, thin mountain air. I took in long breaths through my flared nostrils. The thin air made me feel light in my body, as if I could fly.

We dropped down from the main highway outside of Ennis and turned onto the gravel road that led us across the bright, shallow Madison, where fly fishers stood knee-deep in the water throwing out lines. Soon we came to a green metal gate hung between two huge pine posts. On top of the posts was another thick pine log running horizontally, forming one of those entryways that made it seem as if you were stepping through a doorway into another land.

I unlocked the gate with the combination my father had given me, waited until the van had moved through, then hopped on like a kid and rode the gate closed, swinging it to with a clang, and snapped the lock. Up we went, curving through hills of sage, gaining altitude, until we were on top of the bluff and could look down behind us and see the ribbon of trout-filled water.

Across the valley we could see snow-topped mountains, part of the Madison Range, rising out of the sagey plain. A few more miles and we turned again off the main dirt road onto a smaller road and then in through my father's gate—thin pine poles set in wide "X's," with longer pine poles running between the tops of the crossed logs. It was not a full fence, just a set of fence pieces to give the impression that this was the place one entered, that this was special land, space set apart from larger space.

My parents were both out to greet us, standing on the driven-down grass and sage that led up to the trailer that was their temporary home while the cabin was being plotted and built. They stood like that, a version of American Gothic, my mother wearing a tan Mexican serape, my father's summer-browned and muscular legs showing beneath hiking shorts, work boots on his feet.

My father shook each of the girl's hands and told them he had been looking forward to this meeting. My mother had planned pizza for dinner, she said, just for the girls. She gave them each a pair of silver and turquoise earrings. My father took the girls hunting in the sagebrush for sun-bleached cow bones, which he would make later into a huge mobile; bone art for their soon-to-be front yard.

While my mother and I made dinner, the girls drove with Craig and my father to see the lay of the land; to see the well, to see Robert's Lake, a deep blue hole in the rolling hills, and to check out some of the other thirty-acre plots up for sale on this former ranch. While they were gone a dry storm came up—lots of thunder and lightning, but not a drop of rain. Out the trailer window, my mother and I saw far away the blades of light come arching down out of the sky and we heard the deep, deep echo of the thunder.

Craig's youngest daughter, Kim, came back from the car ride with drawings of the land they had seen. She had created the pictures with crayons and felt pens as she rode in the back of the van—trees on the horizon, a single dazzling angle of lightning shooting down from the clouds; another sketch of mountains rising up, rolling plains at their base; wide-open pictures showing the breadth and beauty of the landscape.

My father was so taken with the pictures, with the miracle that Kim had made them, right there in the van—"Just like that," he said—that he asked Kim if he could keep the drawings. She said yes and he immediately tacked them up on the wall of the trailer. It was clear that the girls liked him. Why shouldn't they? I told Craig later, "They'll never believe anything I say ever again."

This was the way it had always been. As a child, the contrast between my father's public professional life and his private life with us at home, confused me. It happened all the time. I'd be with my mother and sister in public, at the grocery store, say, and a checkout clerk would recognize our last name on my mother's check and want to know if we were related to *him*. Then the clerk would look at me and my sister as if we were the luckiest children in the world, to have *him*, the best biology professor that checkout clerk had ever had, as our father. We'd shake our heads even then, as kids, sensing the irony. My mother alluded once to a woman who said my father saved her life. She was an aerobics instructor who taught a class that my mother and sister took together. I never knew more than this—that she had had bulimia and he had saved her.

When Craig left with his daughters the next day I stood at the gate, at that place that separated my family's land from all that other bigger land, and watched as the van lurched out of sight. I kept waving my red bandana, waving, waving, waving until the dust they had stirred had settled.

I didn't know what to expect then. I stood with my hands in the pockets of my shorts and looked at my booted toes, then lifted my head and looked around me, at the mountains across the way, at the expanse of sage and grass, at the herd of cows slowly approaching. I poked my face into the tiny bluebird house that my father had made and fixed to the gatepost. I admired his carpentry, his knowledge of birds. I turned back to the trailer, kicking a stone or two in my path. I took a deep breath. This would be a good visit—some lazy days of reading in the sun, sweating in the dry heat, clearing brush with my father, chatting and walking with my mother, getting to know them, and getting to know this place.

That first afternoon, I helped my father stake out the borders of the cabin. We indicated where the front door would be with red thread stretched between wooden stakes. Standing there I could see part of the Madison Range, snow on top, some rocky peaks, the rest velvety and brown as a grizzly's hide, draped down the slope all the way to the Madison, that river that curved all silver and glinting in the sun. This was beautiful land. This was expansive, joyful land.

Later my mother and I hiked to the eagle's nest, high in a conifer on the other side of a thistle-filled, cow-cropped ravine on the lot next to my parents'. I pulled myself up by branches and roots to hunt below the eagle's nest for feathers and bones. I found a fresh, full, black wing feather. But it wasn't an eagle's. It was from a raven.

We walked up through the green spring-fed glen and into an aspen grove where my mother picked up a fuzzy feather that had fallen from an owl's breast. I thought of tying them together, both of these feathers, of the owl and the raven, with colorful thread, and giving them to Craig for his Stetson when he came back to get me. As we meandered, my mother and I found a new flower—butter and eggs. We saw a hawk, a badger, a doe and a fawn, and another bird's nest farther up the ravine.

When we got back to the trailer, my mother was excited to tell my father what we'd seen. "I don't want to hear about it right now," he said. She went on to tell him about watching the eagle's nest through her new binoculars, and about how no eagle had been present that morning. "I have a sliver in my hand," he said, interrupting her, adding, "You never listen to what I say."

The sharpness of his words startled me. My immediate response was to rebuke him, to remind him to mind his manners. But I had forgotten, this was the way it was with them, this was the way it had always been. This had been the history, the geography of my childhood and I had been too long away. Had I challenged his bullying then, I would have been the one stepping out of place. And as the week wore on, it all came back to me. The more I remembered about how to behave, the more I felt myself metamorphosing, my very body creaking and groaning with the effort of shrinkage, into a girl of fifteen, into a girl of ten.

That evening, while my father was out scouting territory, looking for old wagon wheels, rusted tractor parts, big rocks, cow bones; looking to see what was what on his new land, I asked my mother if she thought it would be all right to open his fly-tying kit and get out some bright thread to tie up the owl and raven feathers I'd collected for Craig. "No," she said. "You'll have to ask your father first." So I waited. I didn't want to wait. And I didn't want to ask. I wanted to take, secretly, furtively, because I remembered what it was like to ask for something, especially if what you wanted meant anything at all.

I noticed that first day how the weather here was changeable, unpredictable. In the morning the sky might be a deep blue with low white clouds. In the sharp sun, all the colors of the land were stark, bright—gold grass, purple sage, the tan gravel road, the deep green firs. Then the wind would come up and blow across the low sky bringing clouds and rain, muting everything, casting everything in a gray glow. Then, just as suddenly, after dropping only a few cupfuls of water, the rain would stop. The wind would abate.

In my tent that first night, I rolled over and over on my cot, waking myself. I was bewildered for a moment by the bright stars shining in my mosquito net window. I had forgotten, for a second, where I was. But I listened hard, cocking my head, holding still, and I could hear a coyote yipping to the north on a ridge, and I could hear the river from my bed, and I remembered.

"He is building this house for himself," my mother said. My father had asked her if she would like to make an artist's conception of what the finished cabin would look like. I hovered over her shoulder in the early morning as she sat in a lawn chair with a sketchpad on her lap, staring at the open green slope in front of her. She made a few scratches on the thick white paper. It was a pleasant, cool morning, and the soft sun at that time of day gave the grass, the aspen, the pines and the flowers all their best color.

"This is stupid," my mother said, dropping the pencil in her lap. "It's *his* house. I won't get to have anything I want in it." At home in Salt Lake City he had taken up all the space, she said. "I have my bedroom and my bathroom, and if I let him in the kitchen, that will be gone too."

"Don't you just want to share your ideas?" I asked her.

"I don't care," she said. I told her, thinking that it would help, that I knew it was hard for her to assert herself around him. "I don't appreciate you reminding me of that," she said. "Since you have been here you have reminded me of that every day."

That night, as I sat outside at the picnic table in the moonlight, I heard a nighthawk calling in its flight over the woods. Earlier that evening a great horned owl had swooped silently through the camp. As I sat, I overheard my parents in the trailer, their voices rolling out into the soft darkness, hardly muffled by the thin metal walls.

He was tossing her cassette tapes and books and knitting into a pile. His domain at the back of the trailer was thick with gadgets and knick-knacks, binoculars, notepads, pencils, pens, computer hardware, fly-tying paraphernalia, vials and bottles of all sizes, aspirin, scissors, clamps, screws, boxes of Kleenex. Compared to him, she said, she didn't take up much space. "I only want things to be neat," he said. "Everything has a place and should be in it."

I saw what I thought were fireflies among the aspen on the slope below. Excited, I went to the screen door of the trailer and whispered to my mother, "There are hundreds of fireflies out here." He called to me, "Will you knock it off? I'm trying to sleep." My mother looked at me sadly and said, "*Shhhh.*"

I went back to the picnic table and, with a flashlight gripped under my chin, I tried to read. I looked up every now and then to watch my mother move back and forth in the yellow light of the trailer window, doing dishes. When she made a noise, I saw her glance to the back of the trailer, quickly, to see if she had disturbed my slumbering father. She was like an animal, alert all the time to danger. I saw her sip her wine from a small jelly glass and glance back to see if my father had seen her.

My father and I had gone out in the truck, partly just to look around and partly to collect some flat pieces of slate on a hill beneath his property. He wanted the slate to make a walkway in the yard of the cabin. As we bounced along he told me how much he loved this place, how he loved all the small jobs he took on during the day. We were also looking for coils of discarded barbed wire. He was going to use the wire to wrap a tangle around his bluebird houses so that the cows wouldn't rub up against them and knock them over.

As we drove, the harriers, those swallow-like hawks, were sweeping, dipping and diving and hanging in the windy air. "I love this place," he said again, leaning forward over the steering wheel to peer at the hawks through the windshield. In front of us, antelope ran, not witless, not frightened, but racing, rising up and down like a hot wave, their rumps spreading out in dazzling white bursts of sun.

Later, back at the trailer, he said to me, "We're thinking of a name for our land. Mother doesn't like any of my ideas." He said this to me, petulantly, as if in private, but in my mother's full hearing. My mother said she'd like a literary name, like Wuthering Heights or Tara. Or something evocative of the place. "Eagle Bluff," she said, laughing. He said, "I have a name." We waited. "Haliáetos," he said. "That's eagle in Greek."

I had just come in from a ten-minute hailstorm. Now it was sunny out again. The storm collapsed the canopy over the picnic table, the wind bending the pole in half. Then the sky was clear and blue again. I looked out the trailer window at the wrecked canopy and at the hailstones that covered the ground in little snowy melting piles, and I was afraid. I was afraid of what my father would do when he returned to find his tent pole broken.

I decided to fix the pole first, and then later decide whether I should tell him I had fixed it. Maybe he would never notice the repair. It was hard to tell what would be best—secrecy or honesty. And hard to tell what he might do. Would he somehow make the bent pole my fault? Blame me for not preventing it? Or would he thank me for moving so quickly to restore the canopy to its original state? I didn't know. I never had been able to predict, and still I couldn't.

When he returned from his wanderings around the land after the storm was over, I told my father what had happened and he shrugged his shoulders and said, "Oh well." Encouraged by his good humor, I asked him then about the raven and owl feathers that I wanted to tie together for Craig. I explained at length, starting from the very beginning, that I had found them on a walk, that it would be a nice gift for Craig. I would only need a small amount of thread I said, and maybe some glue. He didn't want me messing up his stuff, he said, but he'd do it for me, and he had some time right then, so if I'd go get the kit he would get started.

I brought the kit out of the trailer. He put the owl and raven feathers together in his fly-tying vise and coated the bottoms of the quills with glue and began wrapping them with red yarn. But the wind came up and feathers and bits of colored thread flew all over the table. "God-damnit," he said. "I knew this would be a mistake."

While working one afternoon, collecting brush from around the meadow that would be the house site, I spotted a mouse under the trailer; a mouse that looked like a house mouse, only as big as my shoe. I asked my father what it was. He said, "We'll put some bait out for it and poison it." I said, "Aren't you moving the trailer anyway once the house is up?" He said, "We're only claiming a small piece of this as our turf and this is it."

After clearing the brush, I helped my father fill the fifty-five-gallon water barrels on the hill above the trailer. He'd invented an ingenious system of faucets and hoses to maintain a continuous supply of water to the trailer. When I thought we were done, I washed up and sat down in a lawn chair with a beer. As I sat drinking it I heard my father's voice, just loud enough for me to hear, telling my mother, ". . . she left before the work was done . . ." I put down my beer and went to the trailer door and said I was sorry. "Yes, well, I called you and called you." I said again I was sorry. "The barrels overflowed," he said. "I thought I could count on you. I guess I can't." I said again that I was sorry. "Sorry," I said.

My mother and I were in the woods collecting seeds. My mother picked them for me—lupine, yarrow, mountain daisy—shaking the dried flower stalks so that the seeds dropped out into her palm, then putting the seeds into a Ziploc bag. I could take them home to Minnesota, she said, and plant them there. In the open spaces around us, timothy waved. The sage made fragrant gray-green humps in the grass. We could see the whole sky.

"Just ignore him," my mother said, as we walked. She said again that I made my own trouble. Why couldn't I be like my brothers? They took my father with a sense of humor, a grain of salt. She told me that my father couldn't make her cry anymore; she had no feelings left.

She tried to convince me that all families were like this, that no children got along with their parents, that all husbands and wives struggled. I said, "I don't think so." She said, "Give me an example." I said, "I can't think of one right away."

"When I was a girl," my mother said, "My mother and father hardly talked at all." I didn't know where she was going, but I let her go. I always wanted to know about her childhood, about what kinds of things happened then that might give me clues to who she was now.

"I was alone a lot," she said. "My sister and my brother were in high school when I started first grade." I asked her if she had friends, and she said yes, she and her girlfriends would go into the hayloft to play and into the woods to pick violets for their mothers. They'd ride the threshing machine, getting chaff all over their little-girl bodies.

After my mother's father died, when Ally and I were teenagers, we flew with her from Utah to Minnesota to help her and her siblings clean out his farmhouse and put everything up for auction. During that cleaning, my mother said, she found letters that her mother had written to her father. "She was writing to him about her wedding gown and how it was so beautiful . . . 'I hope I will look like a queen in your eyes,'" my mother gestured grandly and then sighed. "So, I guess they did have romance once."

She told me that her mother once went to the apartment of a woman in Minneapolis, a woman her father had been bringing milk and cream to, and yelled at the woman to leave her husband alone. "My mother was fairly well-heeled," she said.

"She thought that I might get into trouble, so she took her egg money and sent me to the Cities once a week in the summer for voice lessons, piano lessons and drama lessons." My mother used to sing operatic arias as she did the dishes, and my sister Ally and I would cover our ears against what we thought then was an awful sound.

Suddenly, my mother stopped and asked me, "Why don't you ever ask your father about his childhood?" All of this time we had been walking down a hill in the sage, watching out for flowers and keeping our footing among the tiny hummocks. I said something about him not being available, about having neglected the family parts of his life. "You were never neglected," she said. "We gave you everything you needed."

The only things I know about my father's early life are shadowy and come from someone else, not him, and I have no way to judge their accuracy. He was fat as a boy, someone said. That's why he never wanted any of us to turn out that way. He was a rebel, someone said. He went off to the University of Heidelberg to study and, someone said, he owned a racy sports car. He swam for his college team and he was pretty good, someone said. He and his father did not get along. Someone said that his mother and father thought he'd never amount to much, but he showed them. Someone said he was the most brilliant of all his parents' three children.

Someone gave me a box of old pictures of my father, his brother and sister, and their parents—pictures of them when they all were young. One photograph is labeled on the back in my grandfather's meticulous handwriting, *John's bathtub. Bass Lake, 1932.* A beautiful tiny boy, chubby knees pulled up, curly hair damp, sits in a washbasin no bigger than a large salad bowl, a mound of soap suds in his small upturned palms. When I first saw the picture, it came as a shock to me—*he was once a baby.*

After a while, my mother started talking again. She said it took her a long time to realize that her behavior affected others. "That's a cryptic remark," I told her. We were sitting on a rock, resting, sipping water out of my canteen.

"I mean that I drank a lot because that's the only way I knew how to cope. Yes. And if I had known then what the consequences would be of some of the things I did, I might have done them differently. I don't want to be hated."

Each day of my visit, I had spent part of the time helping my father make small improvements to the land. Since the second or third day I had had headaches and my back cramped like tightened wire, making it difficult to sit, to walk, to sleep. The muscles on one side of my neck pulled so severely that I kept my head bent to the right to lessen the pain. But the work, I thought, would do me good.

On one particular day I helped him put up birdhouses that he had made from hollowed-out logs. They were lovely houses, for all kinds of different birds—finches, wrens, flickers. He made the holes and perches different sizes to accommodate the different birds. He was a clever man.

My job was to stand below and hold the ladder, handing him tools as needed: wire, wire clippers, a hammer. I wanted to be up there too, in the trees, hanging the houses. I wanted him to give me a house, or help me make one. But he didn't offer.

I called up to him from my place on the ground that I would be right back. "Where are you going?" I told him I wanted to get my mother's camera and take a picture of him up there. I thought this would appeal to his vanity and also to his need to have every day of the history of the making of this place on film. He said, "No. You're here to help me now. If you're not enjoying it, I'll do it myself. You have to be here. It's a matter of being present at the proper time."

Again, I sat outside in the dark, listening to my parents with one ear, the sounds of the night with the other. I heard a cupboard door open. I heard my father ask my mother, "What are you looking for?"

"Rice," she said.

"Do you need me to help you?" he asked.

"Sure," she said.

I heard him cussing, swearing, pushing boxes around, damning the rice he couldn't find. And then, after he had found it, he turned to her and said, "Is that all? Anything else?" as if she had asked him, begged him to help her, against his will.

Later, as my mother was doing the dishes I heard her say to him, "The water is out." He rose up from where he was reading. The trailer shook.

"Here we go again. Shut the goddamn pump off. Fucking Hell. Shut the pump off." He banged around, pulled on sweatpants. "You could have found a better time to tell me," he said. "Jesus Christ." He put a headlamp on and slammed out the trailer door, down the steps. "Why didn't you check the goddamn gauge? Do you want me to show you how? Do you know how? Answer me!"

She said from the trailer, "No, I don't know how."

He yelled back, "Oh, Jesus. Of course you know how, you did it the other day. You know I could teach *you* to walk through the fucking woods at night to do this . . ." He was roaring his way into the woods, up the hill to the water barrels.

While he was gone, turning on the water tap on one of the barrels, I called to her, loud enough for him to hear, "Are you O.K.? It's O.K. to run out of water, Mom." He came back. He finished his cookies. He read his book. He drank his coffee. He went to sleep.

That night in my sleep I dreamed about a woman. I dreamed of a woman with large breasts who would draw me to her; a woman so large she could take all of me up, all of my fears and desires. Someone who would protect me. Someone who would tell me it was not me who was crazy.

What could I say about this land? That blue flower was like a bell, that yellow flower like a cup of buttermilk, the grass the color of my own hair, the sky the color of my eyes, the color of my blue work shirt, the dirt the color of my boots, and the grasshoppers rattled in the sage like shakers full of beans. When I walked, the crushed sage perfumed beneath my feet. It was beautiful land.

I was in the shower when Craig arrived. I was brushing out my long wet hair. My father called to me to hurry, as if he was afraid he might have to encounter Craig alone, shake his hand, say, "How do you do. Welcome back."

When I stepped out of the shower, out of the trailer, and saw Craig there—bright, big-chested, the short sleeves of a navy blue knit shirt stretched tight around his brown, muscled arms, dark glasses perched upon his head—I felt rescued. All I wanted him to do was take me away, that very minute.

That night Craig had volunteered to cook us venison steaks and morel mushrooms. He'd brought the meat all the way from Minnesota in a small cooler. He'd started the coals, gone through the whole routine of buttering the thin, deep-red slices of meat, sprinkling them with salt and pepper. He looked up from the grill and asked us all exuberantly, a long-handled fork in one hand, a hot mitt in the other, "Ready to eat?"

"Is there a rush?" my father asked.

"Only that the coals are burning down," Craig said.

"I don't care," my father said, his voice flat as iron. "Do what you want."

During dinner, my mother was telling a story about someone she once worked with: a woman who was born on a farm in Kansas, kept captive by her aging father and hypochondriac mother, set free at thirty-five to make her way in the world. My mother told stories this way: she began, then went off in a different direction for a long time, then came back after a while, very slowly.

"That's not important," my father said. "Let's just get to the core of it."

She started again, then he stopped her. "What was it you just said? Let's start all over again from the beginning."

Later during the meal Craig asked him, "What's up for tomorrow? Will we go fishing?"

"I don't know," my father said, bitterly. "You'll have to ask *your wife*." The last two words that came out of my father's mouth sounded contemptuous.

After dinner I sat by the campfire with Craig in silence, and then, in silence, went to bed, and in the bed I had carefully made for us on the bottom of my tent, two sleeping pads pushed together, two sleeping bags zipped together, I cried. He tried to hold me and I pushed him away. I lay naked in the sleeping bags, flat on my back, my arms crossed over my chest, legs straight, face pointed toward the tent roof, rigid. I was afraid my body was dissolving. There was my head and there was my body stretched out below me and it felt putrid and made of nothing but crummy flesh.

I cried for nothing but this, just this, over and over: that the landscape of my childhood had been like this, just this; that this daily cruelty had been nothing, nothing at all, nothing out of the ordinary.

The next day, the day we all were to leave, Craig and I for Oregon and my parents to go back to Salt Lake, there was tremendous commotion. My father darted around, tying things down, putting chairs and barrels and tables and gadgets away, swearing at my mother and me. Craig had moved off, up the hill, out of sight and out of hearing.

At the final parting, my father shook Craig's hand and when I stepped toward him for an awkward embrace, he turned his back to me. As we drove away I saw that he had not even stopped to watch us get over the hill.

Craig and I headed west, sticking to our plan to drive through Idaho and Oregon, then down the coastal highway to San Francisco, then back home. Halfway through Idaho, I turned to Craig and asked him, "What is the worst possible outcome of a mistake?"

He said, "That someone gets hurt or dies."

"He makes it seem the other way around," I said. "That the worst thing is the mistake itself."

As Craig drove, I slept or read. I woke up from my naps groggy. After one nap, I looked out the window and saw land floating past—sagebrush, flatness, hills, mountains. I was anxious to be home, to be in the familiar landscape of Minnesota—in my state, my county, my city, my neighborhood, my house with its backyard of domestic flowers and ripe vegetables.

"Where are we?" I asked.

Whenever I asked this Craig would tell me something like "An hour into Minnesota," or "Between Mitchell and Sioux Falls." Now he said, teasing me, "At Wolf Creek," and grinned as I looked out the window and saw that we were on a bridge and the green sign at the bridge said Wolf Creek and there was water flowing softly down underneath the bridge and trees were bending gently over the curving banks.

"Yes, but where is that?" I asked.

"Right here and now," he said.

PLUM TREE

OUR BACKYARD GARDEN in St. Paul is probably built on a trash heap. Craig and I deduced this as we dug during the first spring, and the second and the third. The winter freezing and thawing pushed up more bits of glass and pieces of twisted metal and coins and curled blue plastic. Under where we put the cabbage, Craig thinks, is an old driveway that was at one time slicked over with oil.

Outside the back door of our house, across the falling-down chain-link fence in the neighbor's yard, is a plum tree. This spring it is full of white blossoms, and it fills our kitchen with a sweet, clean smell.

I am working in the garden today, looking over the flats of tiny cabbages and tomatoes I started on the dining-room table in the house in March. The starts are out here in the part-sun underneath the plum tree, hardening off, getting plum-blossom petals dropped upon them, getting squirrel toothmarks and footprints on them, getting used to the real world.

While I am looking over the tiny peppers and cabbages and tomatoes, the neighbor comes over with a saw. He is a burly, big-bellied man with a kind face. He is out in the yard a lot, cleaning up, spreading grass seed, picking up trash, thrashing at weeds along the edges of his lawn with an electric grass-trimmer. His yard is clean. There is little in it but grass—a few teenage rose bushes in front, trying to get the hang of it, but that's all, except for this plum tree, and a black walnut tree on the other side of the yard.

I ask him what he's up to and he says he plans to cut the plum tree down. I laugh, thinking that it has to be a joke. I notice for the first time that there is another tree, or was, right beside the plum tree and that it has been cut away, so that there is just a stump. I also notice for the first time that on his side of the fence the plum tree has no branches—they've all been trimmed there, so the tree grows crookedly, all the branches reaching out over our side of the fence, into our yard, like some wind-blown pine on a mountaintop.

I ask him not to cut it down. Just wait, I say. Wait until the plums come out. Wait at least until the fall, and let me get the plums, then you can go ahead. He tells me that the tree has been here a long time and that half the time it never has any fruit and when it does nothing eats it, not even the birds.

He tells me that he doesn't like trees in his yard. They shade the grass, for one thing. In fact, he's been thinking of taking down the huge black walnut tree that has grown next to the fence on the other side of his yard. Why, I want to know. He asks me if I've ever been hit on the head by a black walnut. The tree drops them all the time, he says. He's been hit on the head one too many times. I laugh again. Whoever heard of such a thing? Cutting down a tree for dropping a walnut once in a while.

He agrees to postpone the cutting down of the plum tree and returns to his garage with his saw. It occurs to me that he was just looking for something to keep him busy today.

The little girl next door, the granddaughter of the would-be tree-cutter, tells me that everyone loves our garden. "How do they see it?" I ask her. They come over into her grandpa's yard and just peek over the fence, she says.

At first we had only two raised "French intensive" beds, twenty feet long and three feet wide. The next year we added three small beds which we turned into an herb bed, a pea bed and a bed for carrots and spinach and lettuce. The next year, we dug another twenty-foot-long bed. Year by year we ran out of room, so we started planting cabbages and tomatoes and herbs along the side of the house and even in the front yard.

The summer we first put cabbages in the front yard for lack of space, someone told me that there was still an ordinance in the city of St. Paul prohibiting residents from growing vegetables in view of the street. The person who passed this along to me thought the law was meant to discourage know-nothing immigrants from planting rutabagas in the medians.

I draw garden maps every year and put them in a three-ring binder, along with lists of seeds ordered, when the seeds were planted inside, when they sprouted and how well, when they were put out to harden off, and when I put them in the ground. On my maps I draw rhubarb and cucumbers and zinnias along the garage. One short bed bordering the gravel driveway I map out for tulips and daffodils in the spring, and daisies, purple coneflowers and mums in the summer and fall. Along with the peonies that hug one fence, I draw in horseradish. In the other beds I carefully draw in tomatoes (one whole twenty-foot bed), peppers, zucchini, broccoli, beans, and their companion herbs and flowers—petunias for the beans, nasturtiums and marigolds, sage, oregano, and summer savory for the other plants. The herbs and flowers planted alongside the vegetables help keep bugs away.

I only use two chemicals in this garden: Miracle Grow to keep the tomatoes healthy, and Rotenone to get rid of cabbage worms and squash vine borers. But really, the best way to get rid of the cabbage worms and the vine borers is to pick them off the cabbage leaves every day and squish them, and to cut open the zucchini and yellow squash vines and scoop out the borers with a knife.

In every space in the yard we try to make room for something to grow. In the fall the little finches come and hang upside-down off the big sunflower heads to eat. The sunflower seeds that the birds drop we let go, so that they sprout up amid the broccoli. There are ferns in a shady spot by the side of the house where rain water flushes down. And there is a mint bed in another shady spot by the cracking, always wet foundation.

It is fall, and I am making notes for how to harvest the garden. I write:

What's Out There (Do in this order):
Carrots—pull: freeze 1/2, 1/2 in fridge (1/2 shreds, 1/2 sticks)
Cauliflower—freeze

Spinach—freeze
Eggplant—1/2 frozen slices
Zucchini—1/2 in shreds
Yellow squash—1/2 shreds
Cabbage (white)—soup and some in basement?
Tomatoes—sauce
Cabbage (red)—1/2 just freeze shreds, 1/2 in basement
Brussels sprouts—freeze
Jalapeños—dry, pickle

In addition to the above, I make sweet pickles, dill pickles, frozen, whole, hollowed-out green peppers, pickled beets, borscht, cabbage soup, sauerkraut, rhubarb pie, frozen rhubarb, gazpacho, ratatouille, frozen beans, bean soup, onions tied in a string, spinach soup, squash soup. The herbs—basil and oregano and four different kinds of thyme and marjoram and rosemary and sage and lemon balm—I cut and hang to dry in little bundles on the porch.

And then there are the plums.

It is late at night. I have been picking plums all day. I have no idea what I'm doing. I have never made plum jam or jelly. Craig brings in box after box of the plums and dumps them into the sink. They roll out of the box with a rumble; small, round, firm, orange-blushed plums pile up in the sink. I bend over the sink, putting my weight on one leg and, when that leg gets tired, switching to the other. I have on a white shirt, my gardening shirt, which is getting plum juice all over it. I wash the wild plums, then squeeze the pits out. I do this for hours and hours. Then I follow the directions in the cookbook. I make jelly (without skins) and jam (with skins). The hot jars start crowding the table, golden lids shining.

When the jam and jelly is all made I give a half-dozen jars to the neighbors. The would-be tree-cutter's wife, whom I catch in the backyard in her dressing gown on a Sunday morning, seems confused. She is a thin, tired-looking woman. I can hear the years of cigarettes in her voice. "Okay," she says, taking the plum jam and jelly in her arms.

The next year, the man who wanted to cut down the plum tree plants corn and tomatoes along the fence and we see that when the plums come out, his grandkids, even though they have to reach way over to our side of the fence, are picking the small orange fruits and eating them.

NORTHERN HEART

I T WAS DEEP, late August, high summer in northern Minnesota. We had been with friends at Camp Van Vac, a resort on Burntside Lake near Ely, but now they were gone and we were alone. For us, this was a fancy place—cabins with electricity, running water, an outhouse, a shower house and a sauna if we wanted it. The cabin we stayed in was on a little hill. It was made of stone, the kind of house we might have built for ourselves.

When Craig and I were first getting to know one another, he loaned me a book called *Living the Good Life* by Helen and Scott Nearing. In the book the Nearings talk about building a stone house and growing lettuce and tomatoes all year long in their small greenhouse. A simple way of living. Craig asked me, "What do you think of this way of life?" I told him I wanted it, and in a way, this cabin let us pretend we were living exactly that life.

It was called the Honeymoon Cabin and it was the nicest one at Camp Van Vac. It had a big double bed with a curved metal headboard, a thick mattress, windows that looked out onto the lake. On the shelf there were two wine glasses, which the other cabins didn't have. Everything was simple and clean—a wood floor, a small wood stove with kindling stacked in a cardboard box, a candle on the thick wooden mantel, crisp linen.

We had been married some time already, but the idea that we were in the Honeymoon Cabin made me vaguely uncomfortable, as if something was expected there that I was not sure I could live up to.

All day we spent out on the lake, fishing. We had our big boat with the big motor and the trolling motor, which made a quiet hum, and we glided along the shrubby, tree-lined banks, trolling big Rapalas, lures that looked like minnows, except they were equipped with three sharp, shining treble hooks. We were talking quietly and getting our lines snagged. Then Craig had a fish, a northern pike, long and green and speckled with yellow. Northerns fight and twist, not wanting to give up their lives. This one was just like that. But finally we got it into the boat and then we gave up fishing for the day.

We tied the boat up at the tiny makeshift dock in the small cove at the bottom of the steps of the Honeymoon Cabin, and after we took pictures of Craig and the fish, the beautiful big northern pike, I brought the fish up to the cabin to gut it, clean it, get it ready for eating.

I knew well how to clean fish. I pulled my fillet knife out of its leather sheath. I sharpened the knife, first by spitting on a whetstone, smearing the spit around, then rubbing each edge of the blade in increasingly larger circles on the rough gray stone. I tested the sharpness of the blade by running my thumb over the edge.

I laid the fish on the cutting board and with one hand pressing hard and flat on the side of the fish, its belly facing me, its spine facing the wall, I punched the tip of the knife into its white underside. Then I slit the belly all the way up to the lower end of the bony jaw, and took out all the fish's insides including the gills, the long trail of colorful guts leaving a line of blood as I moved it across the counter to a piece of spread-out newspaper.

As I handled the guts, the gills, the stomach, I saw that the heart of this fish was still beating. It was a small, deep red muscle, no bigger than my thumbnail. After being towed on the stringer on this hot day, even after being taken out of the body of the fish that housed it, it was still alive.

From the cupboard I took a small dish and filled it with water. I separated the small beating heart from the rest of the guts and put it in the dish, and there I stood over it, watching the heart rhythmically pumping away, pumping so strongly still, that it made tiny waves in the water.

I called Craig to watch it. I asked him if he knew how this could be so, that the heart could go on beating, beating, beating. He said that perhaps it was chemicals, that it wasn't really still alive, but performing mindless little contractions. As I stood over the dish with the fish heart in it, I thought about how a part of the body of a living thing can go on without the whole body, not giving up, as if it were waiting for the rest of itself to come back together again, as if then it would resume its life all over. I thought of putting the fish back together and setting it free where we had caught it.

Out the window I saw the sky growing stormy. We had planned to go over to Burntside Lodge for dinner, and despite the possibility of bad weather, we opted—instead of driving the van around on the road—to take the boat, to go by water. Craig liked storms. He liked being in them, provided he was safe enough.

I looked forward to the lodge. It reminded me of stories I had heard about resorts in the eastern U.S. in the 1950s—summer vacation meccas with dancing classes and bridge clubs and tennis lessons and cocktail hours and married people having affairs. The dining room at Burntside Lodge was grand, with a red carpet and white linen on the tables. I ordered lake trout. Craig ordered steak. He went to the salad bar and came back with a plate full of buttermilk pudding, Jello salad and vegetables. I teased him about the buttermilk pudding, that he was brave to dip into the mold, brave to eat it. He loved it he said, and smiled at me. I loved to be with him to eat. He loved to eat. His blue eyes got a shine to them and his lovely lips closed around whatever it was he put in his mouth, moist and full. He was a beautiful man.

On the way back to our cabin it had started to lightning and thunder and we hurried, the bow of the boat bouncing in the rough water, me watching closely for the white buoys that marked where rocks came dangerously near the surface. We put in again at the cove beneath the Honeymoon Cabin, and I rushed up the rickety wooden stairs to see the fish heart. It was still beating, more faintly, but still alive in the water, a little red muscle going on.

We were going to take a sauna, and after that, Craig said softly, it would be nice if we could make love. He always said it shyly, as if he were afraid that I would say no. I didn't say anything. I smiled awkwardly, as a way of saying I heard him, but not saying anything else.

In the sauna sweat ran down our faces, and the sweet smell of steam rose up from the rocks on top of the stove, burning wetly into our nostrils. The storm was over by then—there was no risk I would be hit by lightning—and I ran out the sauna door and down the rocky trail, pounded with bare feet over the boards of the dock and jumped into the water feet-first, going down into the blackness. As I came up with my head back and my whole body feeling like peppermint, I saw stars above me, bright as could be.

Back in the Honeymoon Cabin we were dry and warm and alive and Craig came to bed, his lovely strong body naked, and he put a candle on the small table beside the bed. I was dressed in red sweatpants and a red sweatshirt. I had wool socks on my feet and a white-and-red-striped nightcap on my head and I was reading. I didn't want to make love. I just wanted to read and then sleep, maybe be held, but not have sex. I didn't know how to explain it to him. I felt I would be cheating if I let him touch me when I didn't want to be touched. I didn't feel able to open the way a body needs to be open to make love.

I had heard that you should try, that you should be willing. I had heard that after two people have been together for some time, love-making might have to become, for a short while anyway, quite deliberate so that you won't forget its rhythms and joys. He had told me before that he felt like a stranger to me when we went for long periods, weeks, maybe even a month, without making love. He needed to be touched in that way.

He turned away from me in the bed, left me reading in my red suit, and blew out the candle. "What about me?" he asked, curled on his side, his face turned to the wall. "What about me?"

In the morning I got up to make coffee. I stood looking out at the sun on the lake for a while, then I peered into the little bowl. I took the heart into my palm. It sat there in a small puddle of water. Around the edges it had turned gray. I looked closely for some indication of life, but finally it was still.

Craig awoke and made a great stack of pancakes for breakfast and we ate them all with butter and real maple syrup and it seemed that last night had been forgotten.

PUERTO PEÑASCO

A T LOW TIDE there is a strip of sand along the sea that is easy to walk on—a solid path from one end of this Mexican beach to the other, from the resort and fishing town on one tip of the crescent of the bay, to the jagged rocks four miles away. This is a flat, clean place, swept by the ocean, clean but for the organic litter of shells—tiny white sand dollars, the white moons of hand-sized clams, purple-brown oyster shells, here and there a blob of blue-clear jellyfish. As we walk, Craig and I, the gulls keep just ahead, squawking and rising up in a flurry of wings when we get close, settling down again fifty yards in front of us.

Out there is the sea, and low-lying clumps of greenish-brown reef. Shrimp trawlers balance on the gray flatness, their nets suspended like butterfly wings in mid-air. Out there the sky and the water come together. Inland from this solid strip of beach are high, hot, shifting dunes, rutted with jeep tracks and decorated with flotsam—driftwood, tangles of seaweed, milk bottles, beer cans, faded rags of shirts and pants.

Craig and I know little about tides: when they come and go, what determines their force, their regularity. In the office at the trailer park where we are camped, there is a chart which hard-core shell hunters check to catch the earliest low tide and the choicest seashells. We are simply lucky that we started walking early enough. The tide is still far out beyond the reef and we have this comfortable middle way to walk between water and sharp reef rocks and the unmanageable, ankle-deep red sand.

We have come here in March for our spring vacation, to Puerto Peñasco, on the Sea of Cortez, sixty miles south of Arizona. On the way down we stopped to visit Craig's mother, who lives in a trailer park in Tucson while it is winter in Minnesota. We came for that, and we have also come to fish in the sea and to drink margaritas. We have come here before to fish. We have bought fresh shrimp and flounder in the briny-smelling market perched atop the cliff in town. We have bought tortillas and cold beer and limes and hot sauce, and roasted the shrimp over red coals. We have eaten well. This is a place we have loved together.

We are walking away from the resort, Playa Bonita R.V. Park, where we've left our van on a concrete slab amid hundreds of mammoth Winnebagos, those suburban split-levels on wheels that move all over the country according to the season, driven by retired couples from Pennsylvania, Illinois, Wisconsin. The trailers and vans are separated from the sea by a wall, stone steps, and fifty yards of sandy beach. We are walking away from all that toward the tent city erected overnight by college students who have driven crazily down from Denver, Toledo, St. Paul, for their spring break.

All the way here, from Minnesota, down through Iowa, into Texas, through Arizona, I have been building up the strength to tell Craig I am going to leave him.

"Look," he calls to me. "Look. Look." He is bending down, his bluejeans rolled up to his knees, his straw hat cocked to one side. "Look at this." He is holding a bird bone; the leg of a tall sea bird. It is straight, white, smooth, perfect. I am collecting shells I have no real use for, trying to find a half-dozen clam shells that are the same size. I have ideas that I will serve shrimp cocktail in them to dinner guests. As I think about this, I see ahead to the time when I may not be in that house anymore; the dining room table, the walnut slab on two-by-fours that Craig hammered together for our first big Christmas dinner, the one crowded so many times with our friends, will be his and not mine; his for that big house, too big a table for a small apartment. I fill my pockets with shells. When my pockets are full I fill my shoes, which dangle one over my shoulder and one over my breast, their laces tied together. My thighs are wet from the shells in my pockets, and thin, white traces of salt appear as the fabric begins to dry.

I try not to think about what I am planning. I try to forget that from the beginning I never wanted us to be together forever, as he does, as he has from the beginning. I try to forget that since the beginning, even with all of the love, I have felt pressed by a silent, steady squeezing, forced by the unspoken to walk a path not of my deliberate choosing. I concentrate on where I am walking now, on how my toes make small, smooth craters in the solid sand that the water fills in behind me, erasing my going.

What he wants has been clear to me: to be together. To fish together. To be safe. To live. To take care. Together. Forever. I want this too, but I also want my own story: to be separate and apart and brave and full. To choose my own way. He has sensed from the beginning that only a shadow of me is with him. He has been afraid, he has told me, that everything will come crashing down. He has always wanted more than my promise, the promise I made when we were married: "I do." He has not been able to trust me, he says. He only wants to be sure: sure of the future, sure of us.

When we married, when I was twenty-seven and he was forty-two, as I stood silent, wiping tears away from my face with the sleeve of my sweater, sobbing in front of our families, unable to speak our carefully written vows, he said he knew. He was afraid, he said later, that I wouldn't do it. I made myself believe then that I was choosing this path wisely and deliberately, with full knowledge; that I *wanted* to be married, to *this* man. I loved him. Being married was a good, bright, honest, shining thing. A right way to live. But I know now how fiercely I ignored my heart, how deliberately I smothered the insistent voice that spoke to me over and over and over again, saying "This is not right. This is not right." I did not choose deliberately then. I was swept along like a wave, like a tide, in and out, pulled and pushed by forces as far away and as untouchable as the moon.

Craig and I walk until we reach the tent city—lawn chairs, clotheslines, flapping beach towels, coolers full of beer, jeeps, sun-red college boys lounging, their legs splayed, the crotches of their shorts tight over barely concealed erections. Their sunglasses reflect the sky. Their girl-friends, with long, sun-gold hair, spread oil on the boys' muscled backs and smooth chests. It is all part of the mythology of Spring Break, this abandonment, this playful, reckless bodiedness. I think innocently, too romantically, and partly embarrassed, of skin on skin, mouths together, nipples rolled between lips, tongues on cunts, cocks buried deep inside warm tightness, of coming and coming for the sheer joy of it. This is the way it should be, I think, but the way it hardly ever is. I wonder why I don't see boys rubbing sun oil on their girlfriends' backs, and I think suddenly of how full of fear sex can be, how violent, how empty.

My own desire calls me, sometimes stern, often pleading, always insistent, in an entirely different direction—away from all of this, away from the ways I have learned to be a woman in this world since the day I was born; away from choices I did not make; away from this man sitting beside me in the sand, resting, letting me cover him with handfuls of crushed shells. I make a big pile over Craig's feet, over his legs, digging down deep to where the sand is wet and cool.

All the way here, from Minnesota, down through Iowa, into Texas, across Arizona, I have been dreaming, as I have dreamed for half my life, about women.

Sometimes the dreams come unbidden. I fall asleep certain nights thinking of veterinarian's bills, papers I must grade, cereal-milk-eggs-lettuce-laundry soap, and I wake, startled by dreams so full of pleasure, dreams richer than any story I ever made up for myself. In one dream I stand at a mirror, naked, holding her. The backs of her soft thighs rest against my belly, my breasts are pressed against her warm back. My arms are around her, my hands rest just above the soft bush of hair between her thighs. Her hands cover mine. We stretch out our left legs together and turn our heads to look at them, at ourselves, at this expanse of summer-tanned and freckled skin in the mirror, smiling. In another dream I am playing in bed, rolling and laughing, kissing, running my hands over the short, wiry black hair of a different woman. And her hands, the hands that have been stroking my white skin, are the color of coffee. Into my nights women come, like gifts.

There are these dreams, then there are the stories I make up, and like a movie-maker, I bring the camera back again and again until the scenes are right; the scene where she undoes my shirt buttons one by one; the scene where I run my fingers across the bones of her face; the scene by the riverbank in the dark where we first kiss; scene after scene rising from this crater of desire.

When Craig and I start back the tide is up, up high on the beach. We can no longer walk along the firm shore. The water is too deep. We have to walk on top of the hot, loose sand, along the line of sea garbage—a line of water-sogged, half-feathered birds, a leathery sea ray, washed up at high water. It is afternoon. Dune buggies career past us, every one full—a boy driving, a girl beside him, boys hanging on to the roll bar, dipping and swaying with the leanings of the jeep, a case of Corona jiggling in the back. Up ahead there is a commotion. A dune buggy is stuck. The sun-red boys pile out. Everyone piles out. The girls stand back to watch. They are all soggy with beer, roasted by sun. There is much pushing and shoving and swearing, spinning of wheels, spitting of sand. One of the girls is wearing a pink tank top. On the back as I get close I can read the words "Lick it, Slam it, Suck it," and on the front I see across her breasts "Spring Fucking Break" and the logo for a brand of tequila.

The lazy goodness of the day, the innocent joy I tried to make myself believe in while I gazed at the sun-oiled backs of the boys and the long-legged tanned women just an hour ago, leaks out of me slowly, through my fingertips, through the soles of my feet, like a punctured tire, hissing air. Three possibilities? Only three? Three choices for pleasure in your body and in another's? There are more than three, surely, more than twenty-five, more than a hundred and ten ways to touch and be touched, to love, to satisfy desire. For me. For anyone. I refuse this impoverished idea of passion. I know that it is a joke. I know I am supposed to think these are instructions for drinking tequila. I wonder who thought up this slogan, who silk-screened it onto two thousand tank tops. Who makes up these ideas, drawn from the bottom of the deep ocean of some dim cultural consciousness? It's a joke. I know this. But it represents a truth, a ferocious, bending, binding expression of how we live. Lick it. Slam it. Suck it.

Again I think of my own fading, troubled desire for Craig; about the times of not wanting to be touched, by Craig, by anyone. How many times his loving hands have felt like the pads of ghosts on my numbed thighs. How many times I have had to tell him, "It's not you, it's not you, it's me." How many times I have felt sickened by my own emptiness, like a ghost myself, my body a shell, flesh and bone only, my spirit somewhere else. How many times I have said, "I need you to hold me." "Hold me," I would whisper, "Hold me." And how many times I have imagined, when his soft tongue plays between my thighs, that there is a woman with me.

I look down to the water again, wishing there was an easier way to walk. But this difficult track through the sand is the only choice now that the tide is high. Craig and I take turns. First I walk ahead of him, and he puts his big bare feet into my smaller tracks, then when I get tired we switch places and I follow him, putting my feet into his prints where the sand is firmer for his passing. Even so, the sand shifts under our feet, our heels sinking deep, making my calves burn. I look to the shore, where the waves lap at the loose sand. I look ahead to see how far we have to go and behind us to see how far we've traveled.

We come upon a big mound in the line of sea trash along our path. It is a dolphin, black and sun-dried, hard, bloated with flies. Its teeth are bared, its eye sockets are yellowed and empty. Yesterday we fished out there on the sea, in that great flatness, and we saw dolphins, alive.

That day, Pedro Navarra, our fishing guide, picked us up at the trailer park office early in the morning, and we rode through the not-yet-awake town to the muddy harbor and then we rode for an hour more in his long, shallow, blue fiberglass fishing boat out into the Sea of Cortez. We were protected from the sun by a straw canopy fringed with brilliant plastic streamers of red, blue and orange that flapped in the breeze. We caught sea bass and flounder with bits of octopus skewered on three-inch hooks. There were shouts of joy in the boat from Pedro and his brother, Heriberto, "Flounder! Flounder!" when Craig pulled up the first sandy-colored fish, flat and strange, with two eyes on the same side. Heriberto filleted the fish as we caught them, tossing the guts to the gulls and to a sea lion that came popping up, all round, chocolate-colored head and whiskers. Other boats hovered around us, full of tourists just like us. And the guides hollered to one another in Spanish and laughed. Pedro translated the benign, practical conversations. "Where are the fish? Where is a good place to take these gringos so they can catch fish?" It was a good, good day.

In the evening, on the way back to the harbor filled with rusting shrimp boats, we saw the dolphins. As we skimmed along the water in our bright blue boat, dolphins, four of them, suddenly exploded from the sea in front of us, racing us, diving and surfacing, plunging into the water again, and rising in front of the bow. I got down on my stomach and reached out to them. I wanted to touch them, to feel that smooth, blue-gray skin. I had never seen dolphins before, swimming in the sea. The sun came off their backs in watery stars, brilliant and glimmering. I wanted to go with them, wherever they were going.

Who knows what killed this dolphin on the beach. Or how long it has been washed up onshore. I am not afraid of it. I touch its hard, black skin. I am curious. Once I thought that to see a thing alive, then to see it dead, to see it at both ends of the line, gave me some kind of whole story about the world, about this dolphin, about dolphins in general. I thought this was wholeness, but I changed my mind. Instead, I am only seeing a thing, a dolphin, twice—once alive and once dead. This is not wholeness. These are two fleeting glimpses of a dolphin's life—two moments. Stories never really finish. The story of this dolphin will go on even after the flies have eaten away the flesh and the wind and sea have washed away the bones.

I have said to myself a hundred times on this trip, down through Iowa, into Texas, across Arizona, that I would rather die than leave Craig. This, I reason, would be the way of least sorrow. This, I reason, would be the way of not having to be truthful. This would be the way of not having to follow my own desire—to collect myself around me, to live in my woman's body, to touch another woman, to be with women, to love a woman. This, I reason, would be the way of not having to make my own way in a new and an unsafe world. This, I reason, would be the way of not having to choose.

When Craig and I finally end our walk, we huddle into the square of shade on the concrete beside our van and pop open beers and eat crackers and cheese. What should I say? Tell him what? That I want to leave him, he who loves me, for no one, for a woman I don't even know, for an idea, for the possibility of a different life? The absurdity of it chokes me. He doesn't know about the women. I have kept the truth from him, kept it in my heart, and in silence it has grown huge there, filling up my chest so that I can hardly breathe, pressing against my ribs and my breastbone, swelling, hurting, making me act crazy, making me act like a person I never wanted to be. He thinks that I simply don't love him. This is untrue. I want desperately to be two people so that I can stay with him and follow this other path too. I imagine myself cleaved in half, split down the center like a lightning-struck pine, then growing full again out of the halves, into two of the same woman, so that I can have two lives, so I won't have to choose.

What he has seen, all he really knows, what has scared and bewildered him, is what has come of this, this yearning to be split in two, and the horrible knowledge that I will always be only one woman. What has come of this is a smashing anger. We have talked before about parting, but always I have been silent about wanting to be with women, and my silence has spoken violently. We have talked amid the litter of a broken coffee mug, a shattered thermos, the splintered legs of a kitchen chair— all things I have broken in terrible anger, anger from deep behind my breastbone, anger shooting in sparks from my nostrils, from behind my ears. "Maybe you want to leave me," he has said. "Maybe we're no good for each other. Maybe I'm no good." I have been drowning in confusion. "No," I shout at him, enraged by my own confusion. "It isn't you. It isn't you."

Sometime in the middle of the night I wake, knowing I have hardly slept. Outside, the sea is a monster. I peek through the blinds of our van where Craig and I have been lying next to one another on the fold-out bed, naked in the heat. Through the slits of the blinds I see rolling purple-black waves hovering over the cement sea wall, then falling back. There is tremendous noise—tarps slapping, bottles clattering on the pavement, the muffled, anxious voices of other campers trying to roll up their doormats and tie down their awnings. "Look at this. Look at the sea," I whisper. "Come out with me." Craig pulls on his shorts, a shirt. No questions. At the sea wall I stop and hold out my arms and lean into the wind. The chill hardens my nipples and they rub against the light cotton of my white shirt. The wind takes up my shirttails, fills my shirt. I am like a kite, like a bird. I am already wet with spray. I run my tongue over my lips and taste salt. My eardrums are tight with the roaring, whooshing and constant, deep thunder of the waves—waves booming against the sand, crashing onto one another and being dragged back, foaming and spitting. These are waves I never dreamed of—waves so high, so gray, so green, so purple, so powerful that I think in a moment they will wash over me and take me out to sea.

A bright light on a tall pole by the steps illuminates the waves nearest the shore, and beyond that the sea is black. Craig runs down to the water. I stay on the steps. He yells and points down the beach and we both laugh as we watch pair after pair of headlights bounce along the rutted dunes and head into town. Everyone is leaving the tent city. From my place on the steps I watch Craig. He steps back and lifts up his chin to watch a wave crash in, then he chases it back out as it recedes. I think of us like this, how many times it has been good between us, like this, me and him together, and how it won't be like this ever again. I start to cry and the wind stings the hot drops on my face. I hear hissing, the sound of millions of tumbling shells. I want to walk into this water. Go into it. Go. I want not to *settle* for anything, but to take up all this chaos, every risk, all this wildness.

The storm goes on all night and neither one of us sleeps. In the morning, after we have packed to leave, I walk through the hot, still strong wind, through the pop bottles, paper bags and ragged towels scattered around the asphalt of the trailer park, to look again at the sea. The shore is heaped with rust-colored seaweed and broken, sparkling bits of shells. The waves are smaller now, and in the morning light they are gray-green and foamy. I squint my eyes and try to measure them against their hugeness the night before. I turn to see Craig waving at me to come, let's go. I walk back to our van, stop to shake the sand out of my sandals, climb into the passenger's seat, and we pull away. All the way home, through Arizona, into New Mexico, across the top of Texas, I practice the beginning of my story. Through Oklahoma, up to Kansas, into Missouri and

Iowa and across Minnesota, I practice telling Craig that I love him. I practice telling him that I don't regret an instant of our life together. I practice telling Craig that I will leave him. I practice the feel of the words cutting my tongue. I practice the taste of blood in my mouth. And when we get home, to St. Paul, I tell him everything.

GARDEN

L AST WEEK I STAKED my tomatoes. I pushed a tall, slim spike of wood into the soft ground beside each plant, and then, bending into the rich, acid greenness, I tied each thickest center stem up with soft rags, to hold each plant, to keep each plant from falling, so that the fruits grow high off the ground, where they can get sun.

Afterwards I washed my hands, and the smell and color of greenness came off of my fingers under the water with the soap. I could still smell tomato on my shirt sleeves, though, and it was still there on my fingertips when I put my hand to my nose, and I could see it under my fingernails and in the soft creases of my knuckles.

I thought then that I should give you something, now that you were leaving, moving on to a good job in another town, now that our work was done. Ours was a simple exchange and a clear one. I came to see you because I was miserable. It was your job to help miserable people. But I never expected a miracle to happen.

I thought, what I want to give you most is a ripe tomato, a tomato that grew from a plant that grew from a seed that I pushed into some soil, inside, in a small pot on the dining-room table in March, after I had first started talking to you. I had been telling you that I felt I needed to leave my husband but that I couldn't. I had ten thousand reasons, all breathlessly spinning out on top of one another. It was then that you asked me so plainly, "What is it that you are most afraid of?"

I could give you a head of cabbage, purple or green, a stalk of broccoli, a yellow squash, a brown bag of shining cucumbers, a handful of hot red peppers, a bunch of basil, a long purple eggplant. All of these things I started from hardly anything, my back bent over tiny pots of black dirt, specks of seed in the deep palm of my hand, placing four seeds to a pot, one seed to a pot, covering them all with plastic in the end to keep them warm and wet until they sprouted. I planted them all in early spring, after I had first said to you, "I'm afraid it isn't real. I'm afraid these are just *feelings*."

I wanted to be with women, I told you. But maybe not. What did it feel like to want that? I didn't even know. Maybe I was making it up, all that wanting, all that heat in my body, all that desire, all that joy in the company of women, all of that crying and feeling like a stranger to myself. Maybe women weren't the issue at all. Maybe I had everything I needed right here with Craig. Maybe I just wanted trouble. Maybe I didn't know love when it looked me in the face.

What I really want to give you is some fruit from my garden, the most ripe, most perfect, most delicious fruit. But it's not grown yet. It is all still small. It's been a cold summer. A good summer for lettuce and beet greens and herbs and snow peas. Not hot enough yet for the lettuce to bolt, but not hot enough yet, either, for the peppers to grow tall and blossom.

I love my garden. I love planting seeds. I love what I get back from it. For all I put in I get more back. For all the attention I pay it I am thanked over and over and over all winter long every time I sit down to eat. The garden makes simple demands. Water me. Weed me. Stake me up. Watch me grow. Then, harvest me when I'm ripe.

What I really want to give you is something that is a miracle, like a ripe tomato. What I really want to give you is a dense head of cabbage, started from a seed as small as the dot at the end of this sentence. A fair exchange for what you gave me. You said simply, "Feelings are all any of us ever have, ever." And this made immediate, startling sense. Feelings are real—desires, fears, joys. All of them. Real. They are what we have to go on.

When you start listening to the voices of your heart, they demand that you hear them all, and they have come to me all of a sudden now, asking me to attend to them. My own round, red, swollen heart has begun to talk to me. No, wait. This heart has been talking to me forever. It is only me now who has started to listen. *This* miracle I should keep for myself, you said. Then what have I for you?

Like I said, there are no tomatoes yet, no crook-necked yellow squash, no basil, no eggplants. They are still growing. By the time the first frost is two weeks away and you are long gone, I will be picking them by the boxful, making spaghetti sauce and pesto, making gazpacho and thick squash soup. I wish you could have some now. I wish I could give you some now, today, this minute, so you could hold one of my tomatoes in your hand, feel the weight of it in your palm.

GOOSEBERRY MARSH,

PART TWO

T HIS FALL ON GOOSEBERRY MARSH the weather is warm and the
water is high. As Craig and I load the canoe on the grassy shore of
the marsh, the sky is turning from rosy-gold to gray-blue. The blackbirds
that make their homes in the reeds are singing by the hundreds, a loud,
high, rocks-in-a-bucket screeching. Above us, lines of geese cross the
lightening sky.

This is the first fall of our not living with each other, of living separately, of living apart: Craig in the big house, me in a small apartment.
But we decided to hunt together anyway, hanging onto this sure thing,
hunting at Gooseberry Marsh, this thing we have shared for so many
years; this activity that has defined our relationship.

We try in a polite and partly exhausted way to pretend that nothing
is different, that we still love each other, but something subtle has shifted
beneath us. It is something more than the details, the awkward rearrang-
ing of our lives that this separation has necessitated. In preparing for
this trip, I bought *our* supplies with *my* money and brought the food to
Craig's house. When we get *home* from hunting I will unpack *our* decoys and *our* coolers full of wet birds, do *my* laundry, and then I will pack
my bags and leave for *my* apartment. These are uneasy adjustments. We
are unused to being apart. We both feel embarrassed and sad when we
catch ourselves saying, "Next time. . . ." Next time we should leave half
an hour earlier. Next time we should wear waders. Next year let's buy

more bluebill decoys. We both know there probably will be no next time.

But something even more huge and silent has changed. It is hard for me now even to reach out to hold his hand. The intimacy we had, the warm space between our bodies, has stretched so that it feels like nothing. Between us now is only this coolness, as we stand so close together on the shore of the marsh. Something feels terribly wrong.

Even with the high water this year, we have to pull our canoe through the faint, watery channel between the forest of reeds that separates the two parts of the marsh. We both lean forward, grasp bunches of reeds in our fists and on three we pull.

"One, two, three, pull," I call. "One, two, three, pull." We inch along. This is maddening. I can't steer the bow. Because Craig is pulling so hard in the stern and not watching, the canoe gets jammed nose-first in the reeds. We have to back out and start over. I twist around in my seat in the bow and glare at Craig.

"Don't pull unless I say so," I say.

"Just shut up and do it," he says, angrily, wearily, coldly. "This isn't a big deal."

A sourness rises up in me. The nape of my neck bristles. He has never said anything like this to me. Ever. He has hardly raised his voice to me in seven years, not even in the midst of my most dangerous rages. I am so startled I fall silent. As we move out of the reeds into the pond again, I say quietly, "You were a jerk. You should apologize."

"Okay," he says mockingly. "I'm sorry I hurt your feelings."

On the far end of the pond we see frightened mallards and teal rise up, quacking. We know they will come back later. The sky around us now is a faint pink. The day is fast coming on. We open the green canvas packs in the middle of the canoe and one by one unravel the lead weights and string from around the necks of our plastic mallards and our plastic bluebills, placing the decoys carefully in a configuration we think will draw ducks close enough to shoot—one long line to the right of the place where we will hide in the reeds, a bunch to the left, and sets of three and four scattered about. I reach into the pocket of my canvas hunting jacket to feel the hard, cold wood of my duck call. It has always been my job to do the calling.

After our decoys are set and we have paddled the canoe into the reeds, pulled reeds down over us, stretched a camouflage tarp over us, we wait. We hear sharp echoes from hunters shooting far off on other ponds. The first ducks to come to us are teal. They are small and tan, only as big as a grown man's fist. They land on the water and we can see by the tinge of powdery blue on their wings that they are blue-winged teal. We have set some ethical guidelines to stick to, as we have every year. We will shoot no hens, and no birds sitting on the water. We don't shoot the teal on the water, but I rise up to scare them into flight so that we can take a shot. We miss.

The next birds are mallards and we shoot a hen. She falls into the water and flaps around, dipping her head in and out of the water, slapping her wings. Then she sits up, confused and frightened, and paddles toward the reeds. We know that if she gets into the reeds we will never find her again, that she will go in there and die, probably be eaten by a fox or a weasel, or, eventually, by the marsh itself. But I will still see our shooting her as a waste. My heart cramps up as we follow this bird in our canoe, chasing her, paddling fast, trying to mark where she entered the reeds. We look for her for nearly an hour, straining our eyes for curls of soft breast feathers on the water among the reed stems, standing high up on the bow, one foot on each gunnel, looking down from above. I engage in this search with a kind of desperation. I must find her. I must. But she is gone.

"If it's still alive, it'll come out," Craig says. He is impatient to get back to our blind. While we have been looking, another flock flew over and flared off, seeing us plainly in the water.

I feel defeated and sad. We paddle back to our spot in the reeds, drive our canoe into the grass, pull the long reeds over us to hide again and wait. Half an hour passes. The sun is out now and I am sweating in all this wool and cotton underneath my canvas hunting jacket. I doze off. I am bored. I take my duck call out of my pocket and practice making quacking noises.

Quack Quack Quack

Craig rolls his eyes. "Stop it. You might scare them away."

I throw the call to him at the other end of the canoe. "You do it then," I say, stuffing my hands back in the deep pockets of my coat.

The next birds to come over are bluebills, and I shoot one as it is flying away over my right shoulder. The momentum of its flight carries it into the reeds behind me. Again we spend forty-five minutes looking for the bird. We don't find the bluebill either. I want to keep looking. I insist we try again. Craig says, "We'll never find it. Give it up."

The next birds to come in are wood ducks, mostly males. We shoot at them just as they have set their wings and two fall in a mess of feathers and shot, the pellets dropping like hail on the water. We paddle out to pick them up. One is breast-down in the water and when I reach with my bare hand and pull it up by the neck, I gasp. Its breast has been shot away. I shot away its breast. The white feathers are laid wide open, dark red breast meat split open, gaping, the heart smashed, the beak smashed, the head crushed. I swallow down something nasty rising in my throat. We pick up the other wood duck and head back into the reeds. I hold the broken wood duck on my lap. What is left of its blood is soaking through my tan pants onto my long underwear. The warm heavy body lies across my knee. I am stroking this bird's elaborate, feathery purple and orange and white crest, letting tears come up to the surface and roll down my wind-chapped face.

Craig says, "Let's get the camouflage back on the boat, and then you can play."

"Play?" I ask him. At this moment I hate him fiercely. I vow that I will never hunt with him again. I wonder why I ever did. Why I married him, stayed with him. Why I hunt at all. "I'm not playing," I whisper hoarsely. Later, after we have been quiet for a time, I say to him, "Maybe you want to hunt with a man, someone who doesn't cry." He doesn't answer me.

Still later, when we are cleaning the ducks onshore and I reach my hand into the cavity of the ravaged wood duck, scraping my hand on the broken bones such that I bleed, I ask him "What would a man hunter do about this bird? Would he cry?"

Craig says, "No, he would throw it away." And there is a hardness in what he has said, so that I barely recognize his voice.

After the ducks are emptied of their hearts and livers and green, reeking, grass-filled crops, we line them up as before on the banks of the marsh and sprinkle cornmeal on them, in front of them, beside them, behind them. This time I complete the ritual with a sick resignation, as if there is nothing now that I can say or do that will make amends for this—for this hunting gone all wrong, for this hunting when the love between us has gone all wrong.

There is nothing I can do for this now, except take this wood duck home, save its skin, and give the lovely feathers to my father, who will make beautiful dry flies out of them to catch trout with in Montana. I will salvage what breast meat I can from this wreckage and make a soup or a stew; something good to eat, something hot and rich to share with my friends, or to eat alone.

Hunting with Craig has never been like this. My heart aches and I am afraid. I hate what we have done this year. It feels like murder. In the beginning, when Craig and I were first in love, everything was different. I wonder if I will ever hunt again. I wonder if I can make sense of what has happened here. I think now that hunting for us has everything to do with love; with the way we feel about ourselves and each other. The heaviness or lightness of our hearts, our smallness or our generosity, show in the way we hunt; in the way we treat the bluebills and mallards and teal that we shoot and eat; in the way we treat each other. I want to correct this imbalance between Craig and me and inside myself. I want to go on hunting, but not this way.

Part of what hunting meant for us, when we were together, was feasting. It wasn't the shooting that mattered, but what we did with this food we gathered: how we prepared the ducks to eat, how we shared them with friends, how we raised our glasses before we ate, at a long table lit by candles, covered with a lacey white cloth, and thanked the ducks for their lives. Several times a year, at Easter, at Thanksgiving and at Christmas, Craig and I prepared banquets for our friends. Nearly everything we cooked for our feasts was from our garden, or collected from the woods, or killed by us. This, I think now, was why I hunted and why I still want to. Because I want this kind of intimate relationship with the food I eat.

There were some things—flour, sugar, oranges, walnuts, chutney—that Craig and I served at our feasts that we could not grow or collect ourselves. And for these items I would shop at our local grocery store. To get to the checkout counter in the store, I usually walked down the meat aisle. There was hardly ever a whole animal for sale, only parts. There were double-breasted cut-up fryers with giblets. Three-legged fryers and budget packs—two split breasts with backs, two wings, two legs, two giblets and two necks. There were boneless, skinless thighs; packages of only drumsticks; plastic containers of livers. There were breaded, skinless, boneless breasts in a thin box—microwavable, ninety-five percent fat-free, shrink-wrapped, "all natural" and farm-fresh. The meat cases were cool, so cool I could hardly smell the meat, only a sanitary wateriness. The smell was different from the smell of wet ducks and blood in the bottom of our canoe. The smell was different from the smell of the warm gut-filled cavity I reached my hand into when I cleaned a bird. The smell was different from the smell in the kitchen when we pulled out all the ducks' feathers, piling them up in a soft mound on the kitchen table; different from the smell when we dipped the birds in warm wax, wax that we then let harden and pulled off in thick flakes along with the ducks' pinfeathers.

The birds in the store were pared down and down and down so that what was left had no relationship to what these animals were when they were alive. They were birds cut and sliced until all that was left was grotesque combinations of named parts. It always felt obscene to me. What were these birds like whole? It was hard, standing amid the dry coolness rising up from the meat cases, to imagine any life; hard to construct a picture of these birds flying, walking, making morning noise, pecking for insects in the grass, fighting over corn, laying eggs. Hard to imagine them in any way but stacked in their airless cages.

The Russian philosopher and critic Mikhail Bakhtin tells us that the ritual of feasting serves to bridge humans' most basic fears. In writing about banquets and feasting in the novels of sixteenth-century French author François Rabelais, Bakhtin says that in the act of eating—as in the act of drinking, of making love, of giving birth—the beginning and the end of life are linked and interwoven. In Rabelais's novels, eating celebrates the destruction of what humans encounter as most threatening, that which is not us—nature. Humans celebrate their interaction with the world through food and drink, through sex, through laughter. This is how feasting bridges fear.

In modern culture, Bakhtin says, where what we eat is so separated from our own labor, hardly anything remains of these old connections. Nothing is left of our encounters with food, tasting the world, but a series of artificial, meaningless metaphors.

In Rabelais's work, eating is a victory, a joy, because in the act of eating, the body crosses over its own limits—the body becomes part of a larger world. Because of this, Bakhtin says, "No meal can be sad. Sadness and food are incompatible (while death and food are perfectly compatible)."

One year, two weeks before Christmas, Craig and I invited twelve of our friends to our house for a feast. We spent all day preparing for this meal. I sliced through the dense brilliant layers of three red cabbages and set the purple shreds to simmer in a pot with honey. I stuffed our ducks with apples and oranges and onions and raisins, and spread the slippery pale breasts with butter and garlic, sprinkling on thyme and rosemary. We took handfuls of dried morel mushrooms from a coffee can above the refrigerator, quarreling over how many we could stand to give away. I dropped the mushrooms into a baking pan with white wine, where they would gain their moisture back before we sautéed them in butter.

Craig scooped out the insides of a pumpkin from the garden for a pie. He walked to the freezer on the porch and brought back a jar of frozen blueberries. Another pie. He took from the same freezer a jar of cut-up frozen rhubarb. Another pie. The squash from the garden was piled in a cardboard box in the basement. I walked down the stairs into the dark cool, turned on the light, collected four acorn squash, carried them upstairs into the steamy kitchen, peeled off their tough green and orange skins, chopped them, added butter and onions and carrots and cooked the mixture. And then I puréed it for soup.

We were drinking wine and dancing as we cooked. We were full of joy. We felt generous. To feed all of these people, our friends, with food that we knew in some intimate way, food we had grown or animals we had killed ourselves, was a kind of miracle. The meal we concocted was nearly perverse in its abundance.

Appetizer: venison liver paté and hot spiced wine.

First course: acorn squash soup sprinkled with fresh ground nutmeg.

Second course: spinach and beet green salad with chutney dressing.

Third course: barbecued venison steaks, wild rice, morel mushrooms, buttered beets and honeyed carrots.

Fourth course: roast duck with plum gravy, new potatoes in butter and parsley sauce and sweet-and-sour red cabbage with honey, vinegar and caraway seeds.

Dessert: rhubarb pie, blueberry pie, pumpkin pie. Ice cream.

Then brandy. And coffee. And tea. And as we sat and talked, we ate tart, green and red, thinly sliced apples, slivers of pear and cheese and grapes.

In eating these foods—these ducks that we shot out of the sky, that fell, tumbling wing over head, with loud splashes into the cold pond beside our canoe; pumpkin pie that came from a pumpkin that grew all summer long in our backyard garden, surviving three weeks of me cutting open its stalk, scraping out squash borers with the tip of a paring knife; these mushrooms, collected over April and May in the just-leafing-out Minnesota woods full of cardinals, scarlet tanagers, bloodroot, new violets, nesting grouse, and baby rabbits; this venison, from a big-shouldered, spreading-antlered, randy buck Craig killed in November, which we tracked by following the bloody trail it left on bushes and dried grass and leaves—in eating these foods, in this passing of lives into ours, this passing of other blood and muscle into our own blood and muscle, into our own tongues and hearts; in this bridging we were taking up not only food for our bodies, but something that is wild that we wanted for ourselves. Perhaps it was our own power we were eating. Perhaps it was our own ability to grow, to shoot, to find food for ourselves, that we were eating; our ability to engage creatively with the world. We were eating what we wanted so much. We were eating life.

Poet Audre Lorde has written about what she called "the erotic" and its potential to help us redefine our relationships with ourselves, with each other, and with the world. Lorde, who died from cancer in 1992, writes about using the erotic as a way of knowing the world differently, as a source of power that is unlike any other source of power.

We live in a racist, patriarchal and anti-erotic society, Lorde writes in "Uses of the Erotic: The Erotic as Power." We live in a pornographic society that insists on the separation of so many inseparable things; that insists on ways of thinking that separate the body from the world, the body from the mind, nature from culture, men from women, black from white; a society that insists on bounded categories of difference.

But we can use erotic power to resist those splitting forces. The erotic is the sensual bridge that connects the spiritual and the political. It has something to do with love. The word itself comes from the Greek word *eros*, the personification of love in all its aspects—born of Chaos and personifying creative power and harmony. *Eros* is a non-rational power. *Eros* is awareness. *Eros* is not about what we do but about how acutely and fully we can feel in the doing, says Lorde. Its opposite, the pornographic, emphasizes sensation without feeling. Pornographic relationships are those that are born not of human erotic feeling and desire, not of a love of life and a love of the body, but those relationships, those ideas born of a fear of bodily knowledge and a desire to silence the erotic.

Everything we have ever learned in our lives tells us to suspect feeling, to doubt the power of the erotic and to confuse it with the pornographic. But the two are at opposite ends of the world. One is about parts, not wholes. One numbs us to the irrationality, the comedy, of eating animals that are strangers to us, who come to us as perverse combinations of wings and breasts.

I understand the horror among some people I know over my shooting and eating a duck. But while I have become accustomed to hunting and eating wild duck, they are accustomed to buying and eating chicken from the store. Our actions are somehow similar yet also fundamentally different. Buying and eating a shrink-wrapped fryer feels to me like eating reduced to the necessities of time, convenience, cleanliness.

Lorde asks when we will be able, in our relationships with one another and with the world, to risk sharing the erotic's electric charge without having to look away, and without distorting the enormously powerful and creative nature of that exchange. Embracing the erotic means accepting our own mortality, our own bodiedness. Embracing the erotic means not looking away from our relationship with what we eat. And that can turn hunting into a relationship of love; at least not something brutal. Accepting our own bodiedness means acquiescing fully in our own temporariness, and seeing that we are somehow, all of us, deeply connected.

One spring I was walking around Lake of the Isles in Minneapolis with a friend. We were walking fast, dressed in sweatpants and tennis shoes. She would rather have run, but because I was recovering from knee surgery, I could only walk. We took long strides and when I stretched out my leg I could feel the scars there, the manufacturing of new tissue that gave me a strong knee.

We were talking about nothing in particular, about her job as an editor with an agricultural magazine, about running, about lifting weights, about books we had read. Suddenly I shouted, interrupting her. "Look at that!"

She looked to where I was pointing and turned back to me to see what it was I was so excited about.

"Look at the ducks," I said. "All those ducks." As we came upon a gaggle of mallards, feeding on broken tortilla chips a woman was tossing to them from the grassy bank, I insisted on breaking our stride, stopping to stare.

I was fascinated by the greenheads, how when they moved their heads turned violet and emerald in the light. How there was one duck with a broken bill and a goose with only one foot. There was one female among the group of males. Two of the males were chasing her. It was mating season.

My friend and I moved on. She talked to me about her lover who teaches writing and literature at a local college. We stopped again because I'd seen a wake in the water, a silvery "V" streaming out behind a fast-moving muskrat. "Where?" She squinted.

"There," I said, pointing.

"What is it?"

"A muskrat," I said, watching it as it moved toward a small island, its whiskered nose in the air.

I notice everything. I hear geese honking outside my window in the middle of the city. I used to track the garter snake in Craig's and my garden from its sunny place in the bean bed to its home under the house, its entryway a piece of bent-up siding. I watch squirrels in the trash cans at the university. I pay attention to spider webs.

I want to know if I can call this love. I want to know if being this aware, noticing so much, is something I can call love. I want to know how I can say I love the swimming greenheads in Lake of the Isles, when every fall I make an adventure out of killing them. I am full of questions. How can I say that killing has anything to do with love? What kind of language do I live in that allows me to embrace this paradox? This tragic conflation of violence and love is part of what I try to resist in the world, yet here I am, in the midst of it. How is my love for the greenheads, the swimming muskrat, the Canada goose different from the feelings other hunters have for the animals they kill? Can I have a relationship with these animals alive? Or is the killing, the eating, that magical bridging, a crucial part of my love, part of my relationship with these animals, with the world?

What does it mean, that in my body, helping to keep me alive, to make me joyful, to share joy with people I love, is the breast of a greenhead mallard that I shot down on a cool autumn day and scooped from the cold water with my hand?

MUSHROOMS

PEOPLE ASK ME WHERE to find them, and they think that I am playing games with them when I say, "I'm not sure." I only know two things: look under and around dead elms with the bark still on them, and don't look in swamps. It's not a game that has a lot of rules. It's not a sure thing. You find them where you look, when you have learned how to look.

When I first started looking for morel mushrooms, when I first went into the woods with Craig, I didn't know how to see. He had to teach me. He had to point them out to me, even the ones right under my nose. Now when I go looking, I see them where others don't. "You stepped on one back here," I will say to a friend who has gone thrashing on ahead.

You look by strolling, walking through the woods, crawling maybe, ducking and bending, going slowly and looking out, away from your feet. When you look out you can see fuzzy gray-brown baby rabbits shivering in fear of you, even though you mean them no harm. When you look out you can see a fawn folded into the grass, eyes big and black as stones. When you look out you can see a still-as-death mother grouse on a nest, barely visible with her mottled brown and cream feathers. When you look out you can see bloodroot and new small purple violets, scarlet tanagers and the jawbones of deer. You can see the flattened and winter-hardened red skin of a dead fox, the skulls of skunks, the mouse-nibbled antlers dropped last fall by some buck.

You can find as many things living as dead. Going across fields newly planted to corn, to get to the line of elms on the other side, you step along the tiny green rows just coming up, and you can run into a barn cat, all whiskers and legs. And you can stop on the other side of the field in the woods and gather dandelion greens for salad.

When you find them, the mushrooms, poking up like tiny haystacks under the grass, or all crowded around each other, nubby like stones nudged into an embankment, it is always a surprise. To find morel mushrooms in the spring woods is like getting something for nothing: some marvelous thing free. Even as you pick them, you can taste them. They are barky and buttery and sweet like iron. When you come upon them, a lot of them, so many that if you squat in their midst with your penknife and your bag you can reach around you for half an hour, not having to get up and step away, then you feel terrific and nothing is wrong in the world.

Sometimes it is hot and dry and you walk across the corn fields into the next woods in dusty boots and a long-sleeved shirt to keep your arms from being scratched. You wear old bluejeans that already have been nicked by barbed wire, and you rub your neck when it gets sweaty. You hear in the distance the sound of tractors starting up, the sound of insects coming into spring, cows mooing, a horse whinnying. Sometimes there is rain pouring down and you slip and slide and get muddy all over.

Once, while Craig and I hunted mushrooms on a rainy day, he went on ahead and I stood in the rain and watched the water sliding down the smooth dark side of a long-dead elm, the bark layered at its feet, the rain slicking down, bright and flashing. I stood there, wondering at so simple and nice a thing.

When you get the mushrooms home, you lay them all out on a table and sort out the choicest ones for stuffing and baking. These can be as large as your fist, and their flesh is thick, ridged like bark, the color of caramel, and their cone-shaped heads will hold half a cup of wild rice and onions and nuts. You eat those first. Then you sort the broken ones. You eat those second on pasta or layered in thin pastry dough, or folded into omelets. Then there are the rest, which you set on screens on the porch and they dry to half their size, getting better, darker, denser, barkier. When you want to eat these, you put them by handfuls into water or white wine, and let them come back into themselves. They taste like the forest.

HORNED DOE

WHEN WE WALKED into Dee's Kitchen that fall, at four thirty on a frosty morning during deer-hunting season, every head turned to look. In country cafes all heads always turn when someone walks through the door. But there, then, eyes lingered on us just a moment longer than they normally might.

We were an odd couple, Craig and I—a man and a woman hunting together. Not only that, but we were strangers of a sort in Thief River Falls, Minnesota. We had hunted out of there seven years in a row, but still, we didn't live there. We were from the Cities. On top of all that, the waitresses and I were the only women there. It wasn't that anyone eyed Craig and me with any malevolence, we just didn't quite fit in.

We stomped the snow off our boots like everyone else and set our cold thermoses on the counter with everyone else's. We told the waitress that there was dried soup in them, and to just add hot water if she would, please. "That's different," she said, smiling. Everyone else just wanted coffee.

We sat at the only empty table in the noisy, fluorescent-lit room, piling our hunting jackets beside us, pushing up our shirt sleeves so that our long underwear showed from elbow to wrist. As I slid in against the wall, the man in the booth behind me didn't move his elbow from the top of the seat, so I had to bend forward into the formica table. The man talked through me to his pals in the rest of the room, talked across me, past me, loudly, so that my right ear rang.

These were beefy, sleepy men. They sat awkwardly on the bright or-ange plastic benches that were set too close to the tables, so that their bellies brushed the table edges. Their big arms and legs seemed pressed and crowded, stuffed into the years-old hunting shirts and pants one more time. Their hair was uncombed, or combed quickly. Some wore hats to cover up their tousled heads, but others' heads were matted with damp curls. They were hot, all bundled up in wool and big boots. The cafe was steamy with the heat of bodies, hot coffee and fresh eggs, toast and hash browns. Two waitresses, sleepy too, but friendly and sweet be-cause they knew every one of the customers by name, except us, moved swiftly and gracefully back and forth from the cash register to the tables to the coffee pot to the order window, winking and joking.

There was an air of excitement in the room, a carnival feeling of good cheer and friendly competitiveness. This was deer season. It was not yet light out. The day held immense promise for all of us.

"How'd you do yesterday?" a huge man with thick black hair and red suspenders yelled from across the room to the man behind me.

"Better'n you, I hear," the man behind me bellowed back, laughing. "We got two bucks and a horned doe."

"A horny doe?" the man on the other side of the room asked, and the entire room erupted in rough laughter. Someone choked on egg and toast and was pounded on the back by a friend. They all looked around ner-vously at each other for confirmation of the dirty joke.

"A doe with horns," the man behind me said. "We brought it into Erl's station up there to register it and the DNR guy comes out and doesn't know what to do with it."

There was general grumbling and agreement in the room. What did one, after all, do with something as uncommon as a horned doe? There were only two boxes on the form that the Department of Natural Re-sources representative had to fill out for every deer checked in at the sta-tion: Doe and Buck. Nothing in between. Nothing extra.

The man behind me took another bite of his pancakes and a swallow of coffee, then announced, "Freak of nature, I guess." Low murmurs vali-dated his assessment.

I wondered why they called it a horned doe and not a penis-less buck.

Maybe an aberrant female, a doe with an added male characteristic—antlers—was somehow more imaginable than a buck without the proper male anatomy. It made me think about the power of language to construct different versions of reality. The horned doe didn't even have its own name—it was a perversion of two already established "normal" bodies. I wondered too why there wasn't a category on the form, even an ominous "Other" with a blank line after it, for something besides male or female, buck or doe. Surely not everything in the world could be depended upon to fit so neatly between those lines. I drifted into a daydream, setting into psychic motion the events of the day before, when the horned doe was shot.

The hunter, weary of sitting in the tree, knees aching, sees the antlers moving through tall grass. His heart picks up. He swings his rifle around, centering the crosshairs on the buck's upper chest and neck. He shoots. The deer leaps, then falls. The man descends, traces blood drops from where he made the shot to ten feet away where the buck has collapsed in the snow. He waits for several minutes until his hunting buddies arrive, and they waste no time in getting down to the business of gutting the deer. One of them grabs the front legs and pulls the deer over on its back so that the white belly is turned up toward the winter sky, and another pulls the hind legs apart, and the hunter starts in with the knife and sees that there is no penis. There is a moment of indecision and terror. For a moment his world spins like a globe about to tip off its base. For a moment, he wonders whether he might be crazy, or just too cold. How could this deer, how could anything, be both one thing and another all at once? This animal does not make sense to the man. He glances up at the rack of antlers and sure enough they are solidly there, and he glances again at the spot between the deer's hind legs where the proper anatomy should be and there is no penis, no rut-engorged testicles. "What do you know," the man says, shaking his head. His terror passes quickly, but it was there. Even though it disgusts him and makes his stomach tight, he laughs. A horned doe.

The man behind me went on to tell the story of the confusion that ensued at Erl's station when he brought in his horned doe and ended by saying, "Finally the DNR guy just wrote it down as a buck." More murmuring filled the cafe. This, of course, was the logical course of action, they seemed to agree. The man had a permit for a buck, not a doe. If he'd shot a normal doe, even by accident, he could have lost his license, maybe gone to jail. So it made sense that the DNR representative had checked the "Buck" box. That way no one would get in any trouble. And anyway, how could the hunter have known?

I leaned over to Craig across our egg- and syrup-smeared plates, across the white formica, and I whispered, "Is this real?"

"Sure," he said. "It happens sometimes. It's a rare thing."

Those living things that fall into the shadowland between types are too few to count—statistically insignificant, some say. They only exist to prove the rules. But geneticist Barbara McClintock thought the opposite, that exceptions are *not* there to prove the rules, they have their own meaning. McClintock was an outlaw scientist of a sort. She did pioneering work in genetic transposition that threw into question Watson and Crick's theory about DNA being the master encoder. She discovered that in the corn plants she studied, contrary to Watson and Crick's findings, cells had the individual capacity to reprogram their own DNA.

She is also known for what some of her colleagues thought was a nutty way of studying the corn plants that led her to her discovery about DNA. When she studied corn, she said, she "listened" to it. Not that it *talked* to her. She meant that she paid attention to it. She was empathetic. She looked to find out what was there, not to see if what was there fit already established rules about corn and genetics.

For McClintock, nature was not simple, not rule-bound, but so complex that it actually defied human imagination. In the natural world, she said, "Anything you can think of you will find." When you try to make everything fit into tidy categories you miss all the differences, she said. Pay attention to the exceptions. They are your clues to the magnificent, astounding richness of the world.

The very first year Craig and I hunted deer together we went to some woods near Outing, Minnesota. We stayed in a tiny house that had been run down forever, the chimney leaning, squirrel holes in the eaves, white paint peeling, the pine trees practically grown into the wood siding. It belonged to the family of one of Craig's boyhood friends. It was the place he went to learn how to hunt deer. Years had gone by since anyone lived in the place and there was evidence all around of their careless departure—ashtrays still full of cigarette butts, empty bottles of vodka and scotch, dirty dishes in the sink, petrified food in the shut-off refrigerator. Mice had nested in the bed and squirrels had come in and eaten parts of the furniture.

We pushed open the creaking door and Craig looked at me shyly, anxiously, to see if I was disgusted. Already I was rolling up my sleeves and looking for a broom. We moved the floorboards back into place, covering a gaping hole where you could look down to the ground below. We heaved the wood stove back into its corner and hooked it up to the chimney pipe. I got the dirty dishes out of the sink and moved them to a cupboard and closed the door. We swept the floor. I emptied the ashtrays and put the bottles and other trash in a bag and placed it outside the door. Finally, we lit a fire and set up our stove. In a few hours, the place was cozy and warm. The windowpanes started to steam up.

As we ate venison stew and drank wine by candlelight, Craig told me of his adventures in that cabin. His father never took him hunting, Craig said, but he always made sure Craig had the opportunity to hunt. His father bought him rifles and the proper clothes. Mostly Craig went hunting with his friend Sigurd and Sigurd's father and other grown-up male friends.

When he was young, Craig said, there was a ritual the men went through on hunting weekends. They stayed up late into the night in that cabin playing cards in their long underwear, drinking whiskey and telling stories. Then they would wake early, half of them with hangovers, and head outdoors to the hunt.

I asked him if women ever came along and he smiled at me like *You've got to be kidding. Those guys?* There were no girls allowed, like in little boys' clubhouses. No girls allowed except for the reclining beauties on the truck mud flaps, and the calendars of big-breasted women. No real women allowed—no girlfriends or wives, no lovers, no sisters, no friends, no female cousins.

Craig got up from the table and started heating a big pan of water. He was going to bathe so that he'd be clean for the next day: clean spiritually, and clean so that the smell of his human body would not scare the deer. We would go in early, way before light, he told me, laying out the routine, and we'd find a place to stand or sit, and then, he said, "You need to wait there as long as you can." He stood naked by the wood stove with a dish of hot water before him, dipping the washcloth in and soaping himself—lathering the dark hair of his strong chest, the bush between his thighs, the deep pits under his arms—then rinsing and drying himself roughly until he shone in the light.

A woman at an academic conference I once attended delivered a paper about gender politics and hunting. The title, "Too Good a Heart to Be a Hunter," was a take-off from a line in Ernest Hemingway's *Green Hills of Africa*, a novel in which there are mostly men drinking and talking of the size of the horns of the kudu or the rhino they have just shot, and women waiting for the men back at camp.

Others at the conference didn't like this woman scholar much. They were uncomfortable, I think, with the idea of women and guns, and the mention of them in such an unlikely environment. But during her hour of talking, the woman scholar said something that I remembered. What is so radical about women and hunting, she said, is that when women hunt they are taking men's equipment—literally and figuratively. Rifles, pistols, shotguns, guns in general have long been linked symbolically with the phallus, the symbol of masculine power, the symbol of the penis. What happens she asked, when women take on men's equipment; when women adopt the outer trappings of masculinity—if they put on antlers, so to speak? What happens when women, in a symbolic way, invade or take over the *language* of the masculine? What happens when they take control of language or symbols and curve them into new meanings?

What happens, says French feminist Luce Irigaray in *This Sex Which Is Not One*, is that the theoretical machinery gets jammed. The symbolic process that governs society becomes unbalanced. The Word that lays down the law on everything, including sexual difference, is challenged. Things stop making sense. The ideas, the words "man" and "woman" no longer clearly mean what they are supposed to mean.

What happens when women take on the symbolic machinery of the masculine in this way is "disruptive excess." And that's what is necessary, Irigaray says, in order to move toward a pattern of thinking that does not consistently define "woman" as lacking something, as deficient, as a poor imitation of "male." That is what is necessary in order to move toward a pattern of thinking that embraces difference as its own rule—a pattern of thinking that is not grounded in relentless devotion to duality.

It was at dinner, at the conference where the woman scholar had presented the paper on women hunters taking men's equipment, that I first heard the term "strap-on." Someone had bought a "strap-on." I didn't understand completely then, but I got this much—a strap-on was a dildo that a woman could strap on to her hips, allowing her to move inside her lover, and have her hands free to touch her, her lips free to kiss her. Men could, of course, use them too, with other men, and men and women could use them with each other as well. They were toys, meant to heighten pleasure; to serve as fantastic props.

I had vaguely imagined something like this existing in the world. Now, here were these women talking about it, as if it was the most normal thing—to want this and to not want to *be* a man or to *be with* a man, but to be a woman and to want only to be with women.

Someone passed around a catalogue from which you could order such things. "Check out the purple nylon straps," she said. "I ordered this one to match the straps." She pointed to something in lavender, about as big as a banana. We spent a long time leafing through the pages of the catalogue. It was full of things that made me laugh, things that were wonderful and sensuous—books on healing touch and massage, and pages of oils and incense and soft silk scarves.

"When I first used mine I felt silly," the woman said. "This purple thing rising from between my legs!" She didn't feel silly later, she said, when her lover used it. Then it made sense. "I could touch her face," she said. "I could look in her eyes. I could kiss her while she moved inside me." She was *not* a man. She was not *pretending* to be a man. They were *two women* together.

～

In the women's restroom of the English Department at the University of Minnesota, I bent toward the mirror, careful to hold my tie so that it did not swing into the sink. I wet my fingertips and carefully slicked back the short hair at my temples. From the corner of my eye I saw the door open. In the doorway stood a young student—a woman with dark hair and a pale face, dressed in jeans and a green crew-neck sweater. She looked at me, then stepped back and looked at the sign above the door, looked at me again, then glanced again at the sign above the door. I smiled at her. She came in. I left, laughing to myself.

She had been easily but honestly confused, I suppose; afraid she had walked into the men's room, or worse, that I was a man and I was in the wrong place. I didn't exactly look like a man, but I did have on a starched white linen shirt and a gaudy, green and purple, flowered silk tie. The cuffs of my shirt were fastened with silver and onyx cuff links. I had on pleated gray wool slacks, black wingtips, and a blue cashmere jacket. It was all in the clothes.

Kathrene Pinkerton, in her essay "The Bush" from *Wilderness Wife*, wrote about an experience when her clothes made her a "not-woman." The book is a series of essays about her canoe travels with her newspaperman husband Robert Pinkerton in Ontario in the early 1900s. She wrote of stopping in Ojibway villages, of birch bark wigwams, summer camps, sewing circles, racks of meat, men working on birch bark canoes.

"My clothes fascinated the Indians," she writes. "Groups gathered around me. I thought it was admiration until the chief of a small band, apparently a wit, convulsed his villagers by pointing to me and repeating, 'Kaw-win ish-quay! Kaw-win ish-quay!'

"'Not a woman, not a woman,' Robert interpreted. 'He means your riding breeches.' The village roared and shrieked its mirth. That became the summer's joke. And durable. Years later I would turn a bend in a portage and hear a giggle, 'Kaw-win ish-quay! Kaw-win ish-quay!'"

The second year Craig and I hunted deer together, Craig heaved himself out of the small double bed in our motel room in Thief River Falls three hours before dawn, made his way to the paneled wall near the bathroom, moaned and said, "I'm fainting." He collapsed, then, even as I was reaching out to stop him, curling up on the floor like a dropped strand of spaghetti. His blue eyes rolled back. His red mouth fell open. His breathing was so shallow I could hardly hear it. His bare arms and legs were cool and white and waxy and heavy. His head lolled to one side as I stared at him, so suddenly without life on the carpeted floor.

I jumped to the telephone, saying to myself over and over, "Oh my god, oh my god, oh god, oh . . ." and first woke up the hotel owners. "Don't call us," the man said crossly. "Call an ambulance." I asked him for the number. "You know, 911," he said impatiently.

We were hunting with a young man, John, the son of Craig's friend Sigurd. John was calm throughout all this. In his blue Jockey shorts, he moved over to Craig and cradled Craig's head on his thigh as I called 911. The ambulance came. Craig's back had gone into a spasm and he had been knocked out by the pain.

Craig was to stay all day in bed, but he insisted that John and I hunt by ourselves. I drove the van out to our usual spot and picked a tree for myself, leaving John to find his own. During an interval in the day when John and I had made our way back to the van to warm up and drink tea, I complained to him about the blaze-orange hat I was wearing that was a size too big, a man's size, and when the plastic got too cold it crackled and bothered my face. "Typical woman," he said to me. "Form over function."

Later I heard from John's mother John's version of the story of Craig fainting. I had been a "typical woman," John had told her. "She freaked out," he had told her. "Typical woman."

There was a goddess of hunting. The Romans called her Diana, and the Greeks called her Artemis. There was nothing typical about *her*. I am not her, but her story interests and comforts me.

She was paradoxical. She was the goddess of hunting *and* the protector of wild beasts. She was the giver of fertility *and* the chaste virgin huntress. She was the archer, roaming the woods with her band of dogs, in the company of nymphs. She was merciless with those who threatened her or who threatened those she loved. She was tender and generous in her helpfulness for those in need. She took care of small children.

She protected women: helped them in childbirth and kept them from harm.

There is a sculpture of Diana, done by Paul Manship, on display in the Minnesota Museum of Art in St. Paul. There she is, leaping forward, buoyed up by her own power, by the air beneath her, her breasts bare and firm, her stomach and thighs muscular and full; a woman with a bow in one fist and a dog leaping at her feet. The bow, it is said, was silver, forged by Poseidon's craftsmen under the sea.

Artemis Patheos, she was called—one apart, one free to follow the wind, one free to follow the beds of streams and rivers, one free to enjoy the company of women in the woods. She was Mistress of Beasts, Lady of All Wild Things, A Lion Unto Women.

One of the last times Craig and I hunted together was after our divorce. We went again to Thief River Falls, and as usual, started our day before dawn in Dee's Kitchen. There were three of us again that time; me and Craig and Craig's friend Bruce. As we waited for our coffee and eggs to come, there was background chatter all around—who had shot what where last year and who was going to what new spot this time; someone was convinced that rubbing fox scent on his boots helped, someone else complained that his scope was way off. His friends laughed. "Excuses, excuses."

I sat across from Craig and Bruce and thought, not of the pending hunt, but of a date I had been on two nights before. It had been my first real date with the first woman I had really fallen in love with and the first woman who had fallen in love with me in return. We had planned it elaborately, making a spectacle out of it, for fun.

"I want you to wear your boy clothes," she had said. "And I'll wear girl clothes." She wore a red dress and black high heels and nothing underneath that dress but a garter belt to hold up her black hose. In the place we went for dinner, far away from the city in which we lived, no one blinked an eye at us. If they did, I didn't know. I was watching her.

When we returned to my house we danced in my living room and slowly undressed one another, and underneath my jacket and slacks and shirt and flowing flowered tie, I was wearing black silk panties and a black lace bra and it was dark except for a candle and silent except for music on the stereo, and we held each other, entwined around each other, and we watched our lovely woman-shadows moving on the wall.

". . . ?" Bruce was talking to me. I could see by his face that he had just asked me a question, and I had not heard a word of it.

"Excuse me?" I said politely, drawing myself back into the cafe. He wanted to know how I could say that I was a feminist and a hunter too, and we started into an easy, friendly, skimming-the-surface banter which I was not eager to let become complex.

After breakfast at Dee's, Craig and Bruce and I drove out to our spot in the woods. In the dark on the way there the sky was red, awash in layers of crimson northern lights. I climbed my tree with the aid of small metal steps screwed into the wood. I stood on a portable deer stand, a metal platform attached to the tree, fifteen feet up—a special invention for standing in trees with few branches.

As the sun came up it began to snow. The air was still but for the falling snow and the new sun lighting it all up. Around me magic was happening—brilliant, glinting white pieces of ice were falling in geometric shafts from the sky to the ground. It was so quiet that I heard the snow touch the earth. Joy filled me and my mind went again to two nights before, to her hands on me, to her body on mine, to the faint light from the living room coming through the bedroom door and up over the curve of her hip, and I closed my eyes then and leaned back against the tree I was standing in and beneath the layers of wool and cotton I felt a crazy, hungry wetness between my thighs. I laughed out loud at the incongruity of it.

Craig had gone around to walk a deer by me. One came bounding out of the woods and stopped nearly beneath my tree. I shot it. It sprang only a few yards away and fell into the snow. I went to it and spent some time with it, touching it. Craig sprinkled tobacco around the deer. Bruce arrived, having heard the shot. "What are you doing?" he wanted to know. "A ceremony," Craig said.

I took off my coat and mittens and took my knife out of my backpack and Craig turned the deer on its back and I said, "No, wait," and I knelt beside it and touched its lovely nose and eyelashes and got close to its face and felt the smoothness of its hide, that thick gray fur, all the way from the antlers to the white, white, snow-white tail. I lifted the tail, that miracle of a tail, a foot long, a white flag, often the only part of the deer you see in the woods. I felt along the deer's still warm, now relaxed belly.

Finally, I slipped my knife under the skin of the deer and exposed the steaming green, blue and red entrails. I cut up to the breastbone, then down and around the penis, then went up again, and cut through the breastbone, then reached inside the deer and took its windpipe in my fist and pulled, and all of its insides came out onto the snow, still hot. When I had finished, my arm was bloody up to the elbow.

Bruce and Craig tied a rope to the deer's antlers and a stick onto the other end of the rope, and they each took one end of the stick and pulled the deer through the snow to the car. I followed them, plodding, carrying all the rifles. I walked behind the gray, loose body of the buck I had shot, behind the deer body being dragged through the snow. Over a log the deer body flowed, like a wave, up and over, and down, infinitely flexible in its lifelessness.

As I stepped over the next log, I paused with my boot in the air and nearly fell forward in my momentum. Curled next to a stain of deer blood on the log was a tiny woolly worm, as big around as the tip of my little finger, one black stripe down the middle, rust on both ends—a nub of fuzz on the log in the snow. It was curled next to a blotch of red, red as deep as ever, red so red it was purple-black, splattered there on the snow. I hadn't expected to see such a tiny, soft creature in the woods in the winter. How intimate a thing. How wide a world.

COLD

I DON'T KNOW IF YOU KNOW what we are doing. I don't really know myself. As you and I leave St. Paul there is a sense of emergency in the air, a sense of crisis. This weekend in January is supposed to be cold—the coldest weekend of the year, the coldest weekend of the century. Already it is so cold that everything seems as if it will break if touched. Everything squeaks in the cold. Your boots squeak on the snow as you walk back and forth from the apartment to the street, packing the car. The car door squeaks. Our voices squeak. Everything echoes in the thin, sharp air. People walk around quickly, wanting to be inside as fast as possible. They enter doorways as if they are safe at last, as if they were being chased by the cold.

We are on our way up to the north shore of Lake Superior, past Duluth, on to Grand Marais, and then up the Gunflint Trail to the cabin of a friend. I have been there before and I know it well enough—how we look for the fire number on the small metal sign that marks the place to stop and unload our gear on the snowy, quiet, pine-lined road; how we take the car a half-mile farther down and park it among the big trucks with snowmobile trailers; how we put all of our gear on sleds and while we ski we pull our gear behind us to the cabin about a mile away, along what, underneath the snow and in a different season, is a dirt road, but now is lined and packed with the tracks of skiers and rabbits and squirrels and the occasional wolf; how we stop at the electric pole and plug in the lights and we look, joyfully, to see the lightbulb over the sink blink on, and the whole cabin glowing gold in the dark.

When we get into the cabin, everything is icy inside. Brittle. You start the wood stove, and I put on water to heat up. It seems as if hot water is essential. For a long time we huddle in front of the wood stove. You want to leave its doors open so that the fire roars out onto your cold feet and legs. Then we close the doors, finally, and open the damper, letting in lots of air, and we partially close the flue. The fire shoots up the metal chimney and the sap inside crackles and snaps, and the squat black stove begins to throw off flinty, dense heat.

This is the weekend that my feet get frostbitten. It happens when we are out skiing. It is at least twenty below zero. It is so cold that we are shivering as we ski. Even with all that heat in our bodies from moving our arms and legs, from breathing, we are still shivering. My toes feel as if they could snap off—like the finely blown glass legs of a tiny dressing-table deer. I call to you, ahead of me on the trail, to come back please, to hurry, and I ask in tears that freeze to my face, for you to sit on my feet to warm them. I feel in danger. After five minutes the pain goes away and we ski back quickly over the two miles to the cabin, hurrying through the cold.

I want to ski at night with you, but it is too cold. The man at Golden Eagle Lodge says this is the coldest it has been in seven years, maybe more. Maybe the coldest in twenty-seven years. He's not sure. How cold? we want to know. Forty below, he says, but that is as low as the thermometer goes.

How can anything survive? Movement stops. Everything is frozen. We are meant to be still. We are meant to be by a fire. We become still. We sit by the stove with steaming mugs of mulled wine or coffee or hot chocolate and we read to one another. We play phonetic Scrabble. I spell out "duk." You spell "burd." My turn: "zeebraw." We know it is against all the rules to play like this. We burn so much wood that we have to chop more. We chop in our parkas with our mittens on and tow the wood to the house on the red sled, laughing, trying to keep the piled-high sled from tipping over. And everything around us is hard and still. It is such a miracle to think that the earth lives, that it unfreezes, it warms up, gives way to spring and you can count on that.

We have only planned to stay away from the city for three days. But on Monday morning, we know that we want to stay longer, despite the cold, or maybe because of it. So we ski to the lodge, our scarfs growing thick icicles as we go, and we make a round of phone calls. "Yes, we are not frozen and we are having a lovely time. Thank goodness you're not here."

That it should be so cold, that it should be possible to stay warm at all, astonishes me. I remember the story of a friend from North Carolina who went out to get the mail in shirt sleeves and slippers one winter morning in Minnesota. "But it was so sunny," she said once she was back inside, as if the weather had tricked her.

When we return to the cabin from the lodge our faces and necks are covered with frost. We are grinning, with icicles dripping from our chins. Our hats are all white where our rising heat has turned to snow atop our heads. Our backs both have a "V" of white crystal from icy sweat.

Our last morning the frost is thick on the nails in the walls, and thick on the fanned grouse tails nailed to the walls, thick on the calendar tacked to the wall, thick on the window panes, and in the deep corners of the cabin where we've put our milk to stay cold, the carton is frozen to the floor. It is too cold to make love. Our bodies need to stay completely covered. But I descend from the loft and make coffee and bring a cup of it up to you. I ask you if you like this—to be isolated in this way, to be warm and to be the happiest you might ever be, in a lonely, faraway place like this in the bitter cold. "I could live like this," you say.

FISHERGIRL

I AM SPEEDING ACROSS NEBRASKA on a train, on my way to Salt Lake City from St. Paul to meet my mother. We are going to travel the "Anasazi Circle," driving through Utah, Colorado, New Mexico and Arizona to see the ruins of ancient pueblos—Hovenweep, Chaco Canyon, Canyon de Chelly and Mesa Verde. Early in our planning my mother told me that my father would not be able to accompany us because he would not have time off. "You know," I said to her, "this is just for us. Me and you." She said she knew that from the start, but that she didn't want to put it that way to him. "Maybe you'll go on a trip like this with him someday," she said.

It saddens me that I can hardly imagine my father and me in a car together, traveling the West, staying in hotels, eating at roadside cafes, sharing small details of our lives. The only thing we have ever done together is fish. Fishing is the way we have known each other, and slenderly, silently, even then. When we fish, I am Fishergirl, still eighteen and living at home, and he is my fishing father. Beyond these stories we have written for ourselves, beyond these stories we have written for and on each other, the rest of who we are seems to fall tragically away.

There is a picture of me, taken by my brother Austin, in which I am dressed up as a fly fisher. I am eighteen years old, and I am on my first fly-fishing trip to Yellowstone National Park. I stand in the woods, a stream behind me, a pair of heavy waders strapped over each shoulder, baggy at the hips and waist. My plaid shirt sleeves are rolled up, my tanned arms bare to the elbow. My fishing vest is hung with gadgets. A piece of fleece on one shoulder is decorated with half a dozen flies. On my head is a gray felt hat, a goose feather in the band sticking out jauntily. Two long, blonde braids come down over my breasts. I am smiling, leaning slightly on one leg, my hands clasped in front of me. There is an innocence in my round, soft face. A look that says I am happy to be here, this is my place.

Years ago a college friend came to Salt Lake City to ski and to stay with us. My mother had placed the picture on a bookshelf in the living room. He looked at it, took it up in both hands to get a better view, and turning to me with a curious look in his face, as if he had only then realized something terribly important—he said, "It's you. This is you. It's perfect." For him, the picture stilled me, *distilled* me, represented me as I *really* am, as he saw me, as he wanted me to be. Fishergirl. It is a picture that I want to show friends, and a picture that I want to hide. When I look at it now, I feel like an impostor. Fishergirl. It is me, and it isn't me. It was me, and it wasn't me. It always has been me and never will be me.

It was my father who taught me how to fly fish. And it was I who eagerly learned, never imagining that later, as a grown woman, the teaching would begin to feel like a molding. Never imagining that Fishergirl would grow to eclipse me, throwing a shadow over the many selves I wanted to become. I want to know, how much of me is this fishing girl and how much of that fishing girl is only borrowed, made up and put on? How much of Fishergirl is a sacrifice to my father's dream of a daughter, to my friends' desires for an eccentric companion, and how much is my own choice, my own desire? I want to let go of Fishergirl, shed her like a delicate snaky skin and start all over, making her up again, all by myself, as I go along.

On the train I lie with my head on a small, white pillow against the window, my curled body rocking, rocking with the rhythm of the moving cars. Even nested like this, I am restless. As always, I am disturbed by going home to the West, if not on the surface, then in the depths. It is only partly the severe landscape, the rocky dry March. I am agitated in the flesh-and-bone home of my body. The lost feeling started way back when the train left Chicago and is worse now. I get up and move through the train cars, descending to the lower level, furtively opening a window wide enough to feel fresh air on my face.

In transit, between one life and another, I forget who I am. I suffer again from an inexplicable loathing. "Let me out of this body," a voice inside me growls. My soul wants to take flight before we reach my destination. For a moment it is all I can do to stop from tearing myself limb from limb. In the train restroom, I wash my hands and face, lingering over my cheekbones as I dry them. "You," I say to myself in the mirror, "You are a pretty girl. Remember who you are." I look at my breasts, rounded under a rumpled blue T-shirt, my nipples showing through the thin cotton. I feel them being touched, gently by a woman I love. I remember that I am loved. I remember that this is one of the beautiful and distinctive things about a woman, her breasts. Slowly, I come back into myself.

When I return to my seat I pull from my red backpack a book my friend Cate gave me, *The River Why* by David James Duncan. It is a book about fishing for people who don't fish. Such books abound. For Father's Day one year I sent my father a copy of Norman Maclean's *A River Runs Through It*. My father and I exchanged letters about the book. He liked it but was tired of books that pretended to be about fishing and were really about politics or love instead. Once he visited me in St. Paul and on my shelf found a copy of Richard Brautigan's *Trout Fishing in America*, a bawdy, political book about love and sex and fly fishing; a commentary on the quality of life in America and how we treat nature. He looked through a couple of pages and said to me, almost angrily, "This isn't about fishing. This is crap."

I told him, "See, Trout Fishing in America is a guy, a man. It's a spoof on the myth and ideal of trout fishing." When Brautigan goes trout fishing he feels like a telephone repairman. He catches grotesque fish, not beautiful gleaming ones, but fish with ugly tumors and eyes half hanging out.

"It's supposed to be funny and ironic," I said again.

"I haven't seen anything funny yet," he said, shutting the book and putting Brautigan back on the shelf.

I open *The River Why* and start to read. Cate had given it to me nearly a year earlier, soon after we met. Inside the front cover she wrote in the lovely and difficult-to-decipher script that still amuses me, "Gretchen— about fishing and love and other matters of the heart—with great affection this Easter Day, 1993." We had known each other only a month. We had never been fishing together. We had only watched movies and talked, eaten at restaurants, browsed antique stores. She had never seen me with a fishing pole in my hand. She had never seen me in a pair of waders. On our first date I dressed in a black leather miniskirt and jacket. Underneath I wore black fishnet pantyhose and a white, nearly transparent tank top. My hair was freshly cut, clean on the back and sides and long enough on top to stand straight up. I waited for her on the sidewalk outside the restaurant, leaning with studied casualness against the brick of the building, my eyes shaded by sunglasses. When she arrived she daringly kissed me on the mouth in front of passing cars and couples strolling by.

After our date she gave me a note with a chocolate trout attached. The note said, "For Gretchen T. Legler, Fishergirl." The chocolate trout was covered in gaudy, bright foil. The note went on: "You are such a work. So rugged and graceful and raw and polished and pure. You are like a river through me. Everything seems fluid and everything possible." Already to her, even then, despite my leather miniskirt, despite the shades, despite my urban *machisma*, I was Fishergirl. She too was imagining me this way from the very beginning. How is it, I want to know, that we become who we are in other people's minds, and exactly how true are their visions of us? Who invented Fishergirl, and why does she stay with me?

Cate loved one specific part of the book and had marked it for me—a poem by William Butler Yeats, "The Song of Wandering Aengus." The poem for me is about many things, but mostly about desire—the pursuit of a vision of oneself, the pursuit of the *possibility* of self, of joy. It goes like this:

I went out to the hazel wood,
Because a fire was in my head,
And cut and peeled a hazel wand,
And hooked a berry on a thread;
And when white moths were on the wing,
And moth-like stars were flickering out,
I dropped the berry in the stream
And caught a little silver trout.

When I had laid it on the floor
I went to blow the fire aflame,
But something rustled on the floor,
And some one called me by my name:
It had become a glimmering girl
With apple blossoms in her hair
Who called me by my name and ran
And faded through the brightening air.

Though I am old with wandering
Through hollow lands and hilly lands,
I will find out where she has gone,
And kiss her lips, and take her hands,
And walk along long dappled grass,
And pluck till time and times are done,
The silver apples of the moon,
The golden apples of the sun.

The River Why is about a fishing family made up of Mister Fly Fisherman himself, Henning Hale-Orviston; Ma, an inveterate bait angler, and their sons Gus and Bill Bob, both of whom suffer minor emotional problems and act out rebelliously as a result of their parents' constant dueling over the relative merits of bait and flies. Henning, you see, wants his son Gus to be a fly fisherman. Ma, on the other hand, wants her son to catch as many fish as possible on the crudest of baits. She is happiest when he catches a record bass on a rotten wiener. The book is not really about fishing at all, but a setting for a story about love and spirituality and finding your own way in life—finding a way that is your own, finding a path that is not any path anyone has expected for you, laid for you or mapped for you. It is about finding out who you are. Who you are. Who you are. Who you are.

The train is making its way through a canyon along the Green River in Colorado. Hit now with late afternoon sun, the steep rocky walls are golden. As I try to read, I also listen to a family in the seats across from me. There is a little boy and a little girl. The parents are young and attractive. They laugh, they look each other in the eye, wink at each other and consult often about what they should do or will do or just did with the kids. "Case and I are going to the potty," the father says, as they head off down the stairs hand in hand. The little girl is standing up on the seat looking out the window. The mother says, "It's pretty out there, isn't it, with the sun on the rocks?" The little girl says, "Yes, and the river is pretty, too." I look out and see a fly fisherman, knee-deep in the river, and a naked man, lolling in a tiny tub made with rocks to hold a steaming hot spring. Both the fly fisher and the bather are waving at us.

My mother is at the train station waiting for me, nervously scanning the train windows, watching the passengers getting off. But I make it across the platform and have her in my arms before she sees me. I am struck again by how small she feels, even wrapped in a sweater and parka against the late spring night. I am small, too, but feel beefy and huge compared to her.

It is well after midnight as we drive up from the valley and toward the mountains, toward Mt. Olympus, at the base of which my parents' house nearly lies. In my mother's kitchen, around the table, the room lit by the white light of the stove top, we talk. We lean close to one another and whisper so as not to disturb my father, who was not up to greet me, but is sleeping in the basement in my brothers' old room. My mother reminds me not to flush the toilet upstairs because it will wake my father.

She tells me she has started doing something called container gardening. She points to two pots on the table, full of tiny plants. She is always starting something new, always following a new lead. She doesn't let herself get in a rut, become defined by the thing that she does. Once I finally got used to the idea of saying "My mother is a potter," she stopped making pots. Now she does container gardening, watches birds and grows herbs and roses. She has finally grown a perfect rose, she tells me. So perfect, so deep red, so velvety was this Lincoln Rose, that she brought it to work to show it off. "It may never happen again," she says. "I had to show it to someone."

The day before we leave for our trip, my mother and I shop and pack. Not only are we shopping for ourselves, but my mother is trying to get the house in order for my father as well. She has gone to three grocery stores, all far away from one another, to purchase his favorite muffins, biodegradable toilet paper and canned spaghetti with meat. She buys carrots and celery and cuts all the vegetables into thin strips and puts them in small Ziploc bags for his lunches. Then she makes lasagna for our dinner. During a normal week she will do all of this and spend eight hours a day working as a secretary. My mother's life makes me tired. She is sixty-three years old.

My father wants to spend time with me on this morning before we leave. First, he talks to me about his computer, his "PowerBook," how it is the best computer he's ever bought and I should consider buying one, too. He then takes me on a tour of his new inventions. "Here," he says, "is my snow melter for the cabin." It is a big garbage can with a brass faucet pushed into the side. He opens the back of his truck to show me his new winch. He shows me his bicycles. I feel as if I am watching a kid open toys at Christmas. He asks me if I would like to ride to the store with him to get some glue. I say, "No, Mom and I have things to pack yet," and he turns away from me gloomily.

Between packing and shopping, I wander around my parents' house, as I always do when I am home, looking to see what is new and what is still the same as it always was. I open the door to my father's office. Once it really was an office, piled with paper and books, but long ago it was turned into a fly-tying and rod-building room. Now the room has an eerie abandoned feel, as if he got up one day and walked away from it, leaving all these artifacts behind. When my parents bought their land in Montana, my father stopped fishing so much. He stopped tying flies and became obsessed, instead, with building a cabin. His interests now are focused on composting toilets, solar power, battery banks and wells. He is the first president of the Landowners' Association and spends much of his time mediating disputes between city slickers who, like him, bought thirty-acre parcels of the subdivided ranch their property is part of.

My mother warned me about the office. "I don't like to go in there," she said. "I think there may be black-widow spiders in the corners." When I open the door a rich and thick smell meets my nose—a smell of the skins of birds and old, old smoke. The walls are still thickly covered with plastic bags of fly-tying material hanging from hooks; peacock herl, rabbit fur, skins of mallards and wood ducks, tinsel and bright yarn, packages of turkey quills, pheasant necks, swatches of deer hair. The shelves are lined with tidy chests containing pullout boxes of hooks, bottles of glue, tweezers and other small tools. Several fly-tying vises still are clamped to the edge of the desk. And from every surface sprout flies—elaborate streamers, tiny imitation mosquitoes, deer-hair grasshoppers of varying sizes, scrubby-looking nymphs and elegant Royal Coachmans.

He had tried to teach me to tie flies. He gave me a book on fly tying for Christmas one year: *Jack Dennis' Western Trout Fly-Tying Manual.* Inside the cover it was inscribed "To Gretty from Daddy, Christmas 1986. I hope you will find this as useful as I did. You must still learn the basics first." I was twenty-six then. I never learned even the basics. The flies I did tie have all unraveled in my fly box.

That night around the dinner table it's mostly my father talking and me listening. My mother is quietly eating, sipping icy tonic water from a tall glass. She gets up and serves my father more lasagna when he asks for it. He talks about being close to retiring from his job as a professor and how university people are hovering, like vultures, waiting to move in on his space. He feels angry. He has worked hard and wants to be respected. It isn't fair, and I tell him so. In these rare moments when despite everything I see his fear, my heart opens to him. But it never stays open long enough to make anything change.

Still later, after we have spent some time talking about how I will be moving to Alaska soon, my father clears his throat and says, "I'd like to come up there and fish with you." A tiny, cramped part of my heart smirks. Fat chance, I think. I am moving to a new place, with a chance to start all over, a new life, and already he wants to come and fish with me. Already I am going there to be Fishergirl. What about the rest of it, I want to ask him. I am also going to Alaska to work, to start my first job as a professor of English and creative writing. I will be a teacher, like him. A writer. A member of a new community. I will be meeting people, dating, buying a home, maybe even building a log cabin. I will be so much more and other than Fishergirl. I want to smother my own desire to be Fishergirl and even suffer the damage I do to myself in the process, all to finally wreck this rickety bridge that joins us, to wipe away this part of me that feels so made by him.

We started out fishing as a family, my two brothers, my sister and I, my mother and my father. At first we fished from a small aluminum boat at big artificial lakes around Salt Lake—Strawberry Reservoir, Deer Creek. We fished for trout and perch, trolling big red and white lures. Or we fished from shore with worms and corn. We made jigs in the basement, pouring hot lead into tiny molds, then dressing up the jigs with black and yellow feathers. In the beginning we had trout in the freezer. We had trout for breakfast. We had trout in the sink, still wet and gleaming, just taken off the stringer. For years we fished this way.

Then things began to change, and we didn't have so much fish around anymore. Fishing became more about art than food. Both of my parents became interested in fly fishing. It was my mother who started tying flies, ordering great quantities of feathers and thread and vises and scissors and glue from *Herter's* magazine. At first we still used spinning reels, attaching the flies to lines rigged with water-filled clear bubbles so that we could cast them out far into the mountain lakes we backpacked to.

Fishing in our family gradually became more and more specialized, until tying flies and building rods became my father's hobby. My father took a special interest in teaching me to fly fish. For me, as a teenager, it was something romantic and different. I made a transition, a leap into a new identity, that summer at Yellowstone, the summer my brother took the picture of me—I changed from a silly, ordinary girl with no boyfriends and straight A's on my report card into Fishergirl. The fishing will never be as good for me as it was that summer. My father would walk with me to the stream edge, pointing to pools where he said he knew there were fish. He showed me how to cast, keeping my fly line up in the air, throwing out enough line to get my fly to the shaded, cool bank on the opposite side. Then he would leave me to fish alone.

I caught cutthroat after cutthroat, moving slowly down the stream, fishing the big pools and the noisy shallow riffles, too. Sun warmed the back of my neck, the air was dense with the sound of snapping grasshoppers and the smell of sage and pine, all mixed with the coolness rising up from the stream. Nothing then could have done me any harm. When I'd caught so many fish that my imitation grasshopper was frayed, I changed to something colorful and big. I didn't know the names, and I wasn't picky. I'd cast the fly upstream and watch its big wings float quickly down, my body tensed for the sight of a swirl, the popping sound of a trout's lips pulling my fly down into the water. Once, a voice startled me, "You're a natural, you know," and I turned around to find my father sitting on the gravel, his back against the cutbank, smoking a cigarette and watching me. "Do you like this?" he asked me then. I told him there was no place else in the world I would rather be.

The morning my mother and I finally leave for our road trip, my father is sitting in the kitchen with his portable computer and Post-it notes and pens of different colors. He props the computer up next to his cereal bowl and works. My mother reminds me he needs to be where it is light and cheery. He needs the sun, she says, or he gets depressed. But it means there is no room for her. She finally told him, she says, not to put his stuff out on weekend mornings when she is home. He does it anyway, and when she comes in he says, "Do you want me to move now?"

We tell him we're going to leave at seven in the morning. "Maybe you will, maybe you won't," he says crossly. I am finishing my last cup of coffee before we get in the car. My father and I are standing at the kitchen window, looking out at their cat, Bilbo, who is sitting awkwardly, one arthritic leg sticking out at a right angle, in a shaft of dusty sunshine on the balcony.

He asks me if I know how old Bilbo is. I say no, I can't remember when we got her. He looks me in the eye and says soberly, "Bilbo is twenty years old." I am appropriately amazed.

"She doesn't do much anymore," he says. "She likes to sit in the sun and sleep mostly. She's slowing down." He seems saddened by this, but also comforted, as if the cat is doing just exactly what an old cat, or an old person, should be doing—slowing down, enjoying what he or she loves best. The conversation makes me wonder about my father, about my mother, about how much time I have left with my parents. I guess twenty years, maybe. That's only a handful. I can imagine these years with my mother, but no clear picture of the woman I am now comes to me with my father in it.

I became my father's fishing pal. Some mornings I would be awakened so early that I cried as I tied my bootlaces, not wanting to go on yet another fishing trip, not wanting to go out into the cold morning. But later, on the water, as we motored through thick fog, and when I brought home a twenty-inch rainbow trout with a story about how it grabbed my red and white Dare-Devil when the lure had just hit the water, I felt sure that this was who I was. Fishergirl. When I was older we would go on Sunday trips, sometimes with my brother Austin, but many times alone. We would drive up out of Salt Lake, past Park City, into the mountains to fish shallow, rocky streams.

Somehow we became locked into a vision of one another as Fishergirl and her dad. I knew hardly anything else about him except this. For Father's Day I would send him wood duck skins, or trout napkins, or mugs with fish for handles. For Christmas he gave me boxes of leader material, little leather envelopes with sheep fleece linings for storing flies, small scissors attached to retractable cords for clipping fly line while standing up to your waist in water. One Christmas I opened package after package of fly-fishing gadgets. There was a zippered leather envelope full of half a dozen dazzling streamers, a brooch made out of a huge and elaborate fly, a mobile of a trout and flies, a little pad of fly line cleaner, a spool of fly line. Mary, my brother's girlfriend, handed me another package, this one wrapped in lavender and tied with a turquoise bow. She winked at me. "This is for you, Gretty, because you're a woman, too." Inside the box was a bar of scented soap, body powder and bath oil. Mary winked at me again, as if to say, he sometimes forgets.

When my mother and I leave exactly at seven, my father is in the shower where he can't possibly say goodbye. He went in there as we were heading out the door. I want him to be different. I want him to help us carry out our bags, to help load them into the car, to hug us each goodbye and kiss us on the cheek, to wish us good luck and good fun and to stand in the driveway and wave as we drive off into the morning. This may never happen. I can't depend on his changing.

Five hours later, my mother and I arrive at Hovenweep, our first stop. We walk down into a shaded valley, perfumed with sand dust and sage. The bluffs above the valley are ringed with dilapidated sandstone houses, put together brick by brick centuries ago. My mother needs to stop often. Her doctors won't treat her cough, she says, with some amount of anger. They just tell her to quit smoking. This walking is hard on her, but we go at her pace and I am in no hurry. We spend our first night at a hotel owned by a German woman and her husband in Cortez, Colorado. We get a message at the desk that someone has called for us. It was my father. We left an explicit itinerary with phone numbers so he knows exactly where we are. My mother calls home, and my father wants to know where the catfood is for Bilbo.

On the second day we go to the Four Corners and take goofy pictures. In one I am doing a Twister pose with my hands and feet in all four states and my mother's shadow is cast across me. At the Four Corners we both buy jewelry. My mother is gracious and kind to the Navajo women artists. She made pots for so long, and for so long sold them for not even half of the work she put into them. She knows how hard this kind of work is. "I love your work," she tells the women, and she smiles.

Before we go to Mesa Verde we visit the Anasazi Heritage Center. As we walk around the center, my mother coughs. I go from exhibit to exhibit looking at baskets under glass, a whole pithouse reassembled, panoramas, diagrams, collections of arrowheads and artists' reconstructions of pueblo life. As I walk I hear her cough echo through the museum.

At Mesa Verde, we walk down to Spruce House. We are guided by a ranger who doesn't lie to us. He reminds me of Burl Ives—he has red hair and a red beard, a big belly and a deep, friendly voice. His story about the ancient people is full of holes. "We really don't know exactly why they built in this canyon," he says. "Some people say for protection against marauding enemies. But you know, that's a particular idea that may be more about us than about them. These are only educated guesses." He asks us to speculate about the tiny houses built up in the thin wedges in the cliff. "Privacy," someone says. "Lookouts," someone else says. He smiles and suggests that in such close quarters maybe lovers used these huts as places to be together. This idea appeals to me.

At the visitors' center I buy a book called *Our Trip to Mesa Verde, 1922*, a chronicle of four girls' trip to Mesa Verde in 1922. The girls, who were friends and schoolteachers, hiked the whole way from Ouray, Colorado, to Mesa Verde and back, to see the cliff houses that were just then being excavated and opened to the public. Ruth E., Ruth H., Dot and Fetzie were their names. How unordinary they must have been, four girls alone, hiking through the sage, in 1922. I envy them their bravery. I want to be like that. In the pictures they look wonderful and flamboyant in tall lace-up boots and dusty trousers, floppy hats and old-fashioned packs. The trip took them a month. In the epilogue, written in 1988, Ruth E. writes that each one of them married and they all lived happily ever after.

At the hotel in Durango, Colorado, we joke with the two young women who are behind the desk. They are tanned and clear-faced with perfect teeth and wide mouths. Their eyes are bright. My mother asks if there have been any phone calls for us. I joke that we're on the run. "Thelma and Louise," my mother says, smiling at them and winking. The girls laugh. For dinner we eat at an Italian restaurant. For dessert my mother has custard with raspberry cordial sauce and wants the recipe from the waiter. She vows when we get home she will buy a cookbook to reproduce this dessert.

While we are getting ready for bed, my mother tells me that her arthritis is so bad now she can hardly pull on her pantyhose anymore. But, she says wryly, "The good thing about getting old is learning to accept yourself." I keep seeing her in a picture from long ago when she used to be a model. In the picture she wears a black short skirt, waist jacket and pillbox hat. For a time, when we were young, my mother tried to teach Ally and me how to be ladies. She bought us each a pair of white gloves. She taught us how to roll on pantyhose. "Always wear your gloves when you put on your hose," she said, "or you'll put runs in them." Ally and I walked around the living room with books balanced on our heads, practicing good posture. She wanted me to learn to walk with my feet straight, not sticking out to the sides like a duck. She showed us how to turn, like models on a fashion runway.

Most weekends, when I was young, we went fishing. We would drive through mountain valleys, and at every bridge or roadside rest, my father would get out and look at the water. Mostly we were all bored silly, fidgeting in the back seat of the car. But there was also a part of me that paid attention when he would stop the car on the side of the road, walk over to the streamside or look down on it from the bridge, and come back with a report. "Seems high," he'd say. At the next one he'd stop the car, get out, come back, "Seems muddy," he'd say. And again, "Looks clear."

This is one of the reasons I signed on as Fishergirl in the first place. I wanted to be like this—to be interested in and knowledgeable about one thing. His love of streams, of fishing, seemed so complete and pure and mysterious. He knew something we didn't, and I wanted to know what it was. I wanted to learn how to find fish, how to tell a good stream from a bad one, how not to frighten a trout in the water, what fly to use. Mostly I wanted to know what it was that he loved so much. I wanted to experience that, too, to love something so utterly you assumed everyone else was as fascinated with it as you.

I took my fly rods with me to college. I had two, both safely traveling in black plastic tubes, with my name on them in gold tape. Gretchen T. Legler. My father had made both of the rods for me and the carrying tubes. I stored the rods in my dorm room, in the back of the closet. No one I knew at college wanted to fish. But they all liked the idea that I had fly rods in the back of my closet. It made me interesting. A professor of mine flattered me by giving me a fly tying kit—a big metal box filled with clear plastic drawers. In each drawer was something new—hooks of different sizes, colored thread and tinsel, feathers, hair, yarn and glue. He had bought it thinking he'd get into fly fishing, he said. But he had never opened it. I have moved the kit around with me to six different homes and apartments. I've never used it either.

One weekend in college I could not bear the city a moment longer and headed off to the rolling green hills of southern Minnesota to fish. I did some research and got the trout stream maps from the Minnesota Department of Natural Resources. I thought I knew exactly where I was going. As I drove along the dirt roads in the hot and heavy humid air, I slowly passed a black Amish buggy. Two little boys in flat straw hats grinned and waved at me. Their father, driving, nodded as I passed them. I was proud and feeling independent, feeling like Fishergirl.

I drove around all day looking for the stream that looked just right— something wide and deep, like the streams in Utah and Wyoming. But these streams confused me. They were all thin and muddy and covered over by trees. How would you fish a stream like this? A kind of indecision had seized me. I realized that this was no fun at all. The whole activity lost its meaning. I drove back to the city, to my dorm room and my books. I had not even wetted my line. I felt somehow stupid and false, as if I wasn't cut out for this at all, as if without my father by my side, I was no Fishergirl at all. I wanted to be solid unto myself and, instead, I felt full of holes.

When my mother and I leave Durango, we head off in the wrong direction. All the while we are driving happily and talking. We talk about her pottery. She tries to explain to me that the pots themselves were never her goal. That the whole thing was about process. And when she stopped making pots, it wasn't as if she had stopped being herself. She just moved on to something new.

Pottery defined her for me for so long. She was always in the garage working with a mound of clay on her wheel, loading her kiln, or in the kitchen with a pot on the table, rubbing the outside with a wooden spoon to make it shine. Her pots were mostly hand-built. She was trying, she said, to replicate Anasazi methods and designs. There was always clay on the doorknobs, clay on the phone.

Now she's stopped. She tells me that my father keeps asking her when she'll get back to pottery. "Maybe never," she tells him. She says to him, "I'm just not interested anymore." Now the garage is full of his tools and gadgets, and the kiln is on the back porch under a tarp. "What do you mean you're not interested anymore?" he asks her. She tells him that she is changing, that's it, and that he has changed, too; after all, he quit tying flies.

My mother and I get to Silverton before I realize we are going the wrong way. I tell her sheepishly that we need to turn around. She heads back up over the pass on the curving road we've just come down. It is cold on top of the pass. There is a lot of snow. It is beautiful. She tells me that she dreams about being on an endless road and coming to crevasse after crevasse and turning around. "This has something to do with life," she says, her eyes on the road, both hands on the wheel.

We talk about my being a lesbian. She tells me that since I told her this about myself she has discovered that everywhere she turns there is a lesbian or a gay man—an author, a friend, a movie star and ordinary people, too. The letter I wrote to my parents, in which I revealed the reason I had left my husband, was boring and full of platitudes. It was full of short, declarative sentences. I had been careful with every word, every phrase. I wanted them both to understand plainly, with no flourishes, what had happened to me, how I had changed, how I had emerged. The letter had nothing in it of the joy I felt at the time. I was unaccustomed to the language of joy. The very word "joy" felt awkward in my hands. I had hardly a vocabulary to express myself, whereas I had practiced for years the language of grief. "I am so happy," I told my parents in the letter. That is the word I repeated over and over and over. Happy. Happy. Happy. Only my mother understood. She turns to me now in the car and says, "You seem happier."

My mother telephoned as soon as she got my letter. I was sitting at the kitchen table by an open window. There was sun shining in. Cate sat next to me in a chair, holding my hand with both of hers. My mother did not say much. I had to chip loose what I wanted from her. I asked, "Are you surprised?"

"Yes and no."

"Are you sad?"

"Yes."

"Why?"

"The world is so unpredictable. Things hardly ever go anymore as you expect."

I was quiet.

"I have been thinking about how much it takes to raise a child," she said. "And I think we always did the right thing, but maybe not." She paused and then said, "I know we always did stop for ice cream."

Afterward, exhausted, I lay down in bed next to Cate and we slept. It had been easier than I had imagined, telling my mother. She had said all of the right things. "We still love you," she had said. But still, I was overcome by a deep weariness all mixed up with sadness and a clear sense of being suddenly released from a great, sagging weight. I was free. Free. Free of something. What? Free to do what? Be what? In my sleep I dreamed of my sister, Ally. I dreamed I was holding her hand, and I woke with Cate's hand in mine. I slept again, and awoke when I heard some-one call me by my name. Still, Cate was sound asleep beside me. "Gretchen," the voice said, only once and very clear.

As my mother drives, I ask her why my father never called me about the letter. "I'll tell you, but you won't like it," she says. "He said he didn't care as long you didn't tell everybody. He thinks sexual proclivities are private things."

"Oh," I say.

"And he never read your letter."

My heart lands like a stone in my chest.

"He worries about you," she tells me, "that it will be hard for you to be happy like this. That it will be hard for you to get a job." I laugh. My life has never been this easy. I have finally claimed space for myself against the forces that work to keep us all from knowing who we are; the forces that keep us pasting ourselves together from the fragments of other people's desires. Of course, I think, he would never read my letter. He wouldn't understand it, and it would frighten him.

There is another picture of me fly fishing. This time in color, taken by Craig when we were still married. In it I am wearing a bright-red flannel shirt. On my head is the same old hat, adorned with a different feather—still long and gray, something I picked up along a stream or in the woods, vowing that I'd place it in my hat and never forget where it came from. My fly rod is tucked under one arm, and in my other hand I am holding a shining, flickering cutthroat trout upside down by the tail. I learned all this from my father. When you get the fish, you pull in line enough so you have the fish under control; then you pull your bandana from your vest, wet it, and taking the fish gently by its strong tail, lift it out of the water and carefully take the fly out of its mouth. Before you had even started to fish, you had clipped the barb off of the hook so that the fish's mouth would be hurt as little as possible. Then you let the fish go, first holding it by its tail in the stream until it has got its wits back and can swim away.

On the day this picture was taken, Craig caught an extraordinary fish. We had seen it lurking in the shade under the opposite bank, and Craig worked all morning to get it to strike. He played the fish too long, however, and by the time it was unhooked the fish was frail. And when he released it, the fish turned over on its back, its white belly open to the sky. Craig was cradling it in his palms in the water when my father appeared around the bend. He showed Craig how to resuscitate a fish by moving it slowly back and forth in the water, forcing oxygen into its gills. He did this with his big, intelligent hands until the fish flipped its tail and swam strongly upstream. Craig told me, jokingly, that he was lucky. He only caught fish when my father was there to see it. He seemed to understand so quickly something I had felt painfully all my life, that being good at fishing somehow wins my father's respect.

On one of our first dates, I took Craig to Hay Creek, a tiny trout stream in southern Minnesota. I wanted to impress Craig, so in preparation for the trip I called my father for advice. I told him that I didn't know how to fish these little Minnesota streams, and he told me I should use wet flies. Nymphs. He sent me a gift of a small packet of fluorescent green and orange "strike indicators," bits of colored foam tape you tear off and stick on your leader when you are using a nymph. You watch the strike indicator and when it stops moving, odds are your nymph is being nibbled by a trout. I hear his voice, "My nymph fishing improved about fifty percent when I started using strike indicators."

On that trip, Craig and I fished in ankle-deep water, catching two small trout; then we spread out a blanket beside the stream for our lunch. We played, putting grapes in each other's mouths, feeding each other sliced apples and cheese, and then started to kiss, finally making slow love in the tall grass. I saw sky over his back. I heard birds and the water. I smelled warm dust from the road. We washed naked in the cold stream, and I teased him that this was a risky idea he had had, what with the road so near. "It was your idea too," he said, smiling.

Craig took a picture of me on that trip that he later had a friend of ours make into a watercolor painting. I often think that it is only partly an image of me that emerged on that photographic paper; the rest is Craig's vision of me, fed by his love. The painting hung above our bed, until after we divorced and Craig gave it back to me—my shining face and blue, blue eyes, a green shirt, a green hat and a yellow daisy in the hatband. In the painting, I look like a wood sprite. I look like Fishergirl.

My mother and I are winding our way toward Chaco Canyon on the third day of our trip. We take a thin, rutted dirt road, so narrow in places and hemmed in by red rock that I wonder if the car will fit through. It is early in the season and the road hasn't been graded yet. All the ruins here are in the canyon bottom, not up in the cliffs. Pueblo Bonito, the largest ruin in the canyon, is said to have been a mecca, a cultural and political center, crawling with people, surrounded by farms. There are roads carved in the sandstone, going up over the red rock sides of the canyon and leading to other pueblos. One story is that Pueblo Bonito got too large. There were a couple of bad years. Everyone died or moved. I want to know where the people went. I want to know what happened to their lives, their individual, private lives.

I tell my mother I am finally beginning to figure out my life. I am realizing that there are doors that will not always be open to me. I feel as if I am becoming wise, that my youth is ending. She looks at me and says quietly, "People talk about finding the meaning of life. People used to know what the meaning of life was—a job and a place to live and enough to eat. Life has gotten so complicated."

We talk about my father. She tells me that before my visit, my father asked especially for her to sit and talk to him about something important. They sat, one on each end of the kitchen table, and he told her that he was worried about my visit. He was worried that I would be difficult. Difficult. I would ask hard questions. I would rebel in small, insignificant ways. I would frustrate him by sleeping in late in the mornings, waking only after he had left the house, by staying up late, talking with my mother in the kitchen long after he had gone to bed, and by crying. "He always makes you cry," my mother has said on other visits. "I hope he doesn't make you cry. You don't have to let him make you cry."

My mother tells me that my father wants to spend time with me. "He wants to spend time with you *alone*," she says. "He tells me that he hasn't spent time with you alone in three years." Alone for what, I want to ask. Even when we are alone together, the space between us is like a vast canyon that our voices barely carry across. The last time we were alone together, we went fishing at my parents' cabin in Montana. We packed lunches and water and hiked down the steep slope to the Madison River. As we put on our wading gear and tied on flies, he talked to me about my mother. He said he loved her and didn't want her to die before he did.

"Have you told her that?" I asked.

"Not in so many words," he said. "There's no doubt in my mind. Unless I get hit by a car, I will outlive your mother."

He left me at the first pool. I watched him tromping downstream in his waders and fishing vest, his rod tip bobbing as he stepped over grassy hummocks, until he disappeared around the first big bend. I tied on a fly, something big with white wings that I could see easily in the fast water, and listlessly cast out and drew in line for two hours. My father, I knew, would be catching fish. He would be taking up netfuls of river water, scientifically determining the insects the fish were eating, and then finding (or tying) an exact match.

When he came back to join me at lunchtime, he found me lying in the sun, reading a mystery novel. Beside me I had a stack of reeds I had collected for my mother, who wanted them to thatch the roofs of the birdhouses my father had been building from hollowed-out logs. He set his rod down in the grass and took a sip of water. He asked me, "Have you ever thought we were rich?" I said no. "Well, we're not rich. We never have been. But Mother has done an incredible job managing our finances, so we have a good ratio of income to outflow and a good retirement." I asked if he had told her that. "Not in so many words," he said. "I'm tempted to ask her to show me how to do it. I'm going to need to know." I want to ask him with what words or what actions he *has* told her that he loves her. I want to ask him if he loves me.

On the fourth day my mother and I leave Gallup and go to Window Rock on the Navajo Reservation. We stop at the Hubbell Trading Post and visit a shop where Navajo women are weaving. My mother wants to talk to them, but they only smile at her. She looks at a young woman standing nearby and says to her, "I guess I don't speak their language. Can you ask them how long it takes them to weave one of these rugs?" The young woman says something to the older women, and then turns to my mother and says, "These are women in their seventies. They only speak *Dine*. They never went to school. They were old-fashioned and stayed home all of their lives, you know. It takes them hundreds of hours to weave a blanket." When we leave, my mother thanks the old weavers and the young woman who was her interpreter. My mother is one of the nicest people I know.

In the beginning I liked that fly fishing with my father made me feel somehow superior to people who fished with spinning gear and bait. I felt as if I had evolved into a more refined and more intelligent creature when I learned to fly fish. I would laugh at the jokes my father would make about hayseeds who fished with corn and cheese balls. But after a while the jokes didn't seem funny anymore. On one particular trip I remember feeling ashamed and putting the shame in my pocket like a shell or a tiny pinecone.

My father and brother and I had set out on an already hot, dry morning for the lower part of Slough Creek in Yellowstone. We had taken a short cut over a steep hill, into the woods, where we often saw moose and deer. Far away, up higher on the green meadows, we had heard elk bugle. Along the way we met a horse-drawn wagon taking this route to a dude ranch north of the park. We got to the stream, and there was no one there yet. As we sat on a log by the very first pool, quiet at that time of day, still and amber-colored, we peeled off our boots and wool socks and put on waders and wading shoes and got our fly rods set. I was missing something, as always, and had to ask for it—some tippet, some leader, maybe a few extra flies. My father handed them over impatiently, as if to say, you're old enough now to have your fishing vest in order.

As we were preparing to fish, a father and son arrived, talking loudly, breaking the still. And my father muttered under his voice as they moved away, walking merrily along the high grassy bank, that they would scare the fish, that they shouldn't be allowed here with their spinning gear and flashing, hook-heavy lures. I told him in the kind of controlled, angry voice in which I was learning to speak with him, "It isn't our stream." He looked at me and smiled and said, "Yes, it is." Instead of feeling fine and laughing, I just felt snobbish, and I knew it wasn't right.

We are headed to Canyon de Chelly. My mother describes a movie to me about a woman and a man who fall in love. He's an ex-con. The man and woman kiss in the movie. It is their first kiss, tentative and full of passion. She could feel the passion, she says, the electricity. She hasn't felt that way in a long time.

"Is that what you feel?" she asks me, tentatively.

"You mean with a woman?"

"Yes," she says.

"Yes," I answer. "Now more than ever before." I try to explain this to her. "It wasn't that I never had great sex with men," I say. "It's that with them, with men, I was never fully present in my own body." She tells me that she is surprised and a little embarassed that I talk so easily about sex.

At Canyon de Chelly we walk down into the wash to see the White House Ruins. I keep handing my mother my water bottle and urging her to drink. "Water is good for you," I say. It is a steep walk, and she goes slowly. At the bottom there is thin spring grass and a hogan, and red walls rising up to blue cloudless sky. We walk along the wash in the deep sand to the ruins, where there are other people who have come down in four-wheel-drive vehicles with Navajo guides.

At the ruins some women have spread out blankets and are selling jewelry. I buy a silver medallion, shaped like the sun, on a leather string. Coming up from the bottom of the canyon, my mother takes a picture of me in my bluejeans and ribbed, sleeveless undershirt, the medallion around my neck. In the picture I imagine coming from this shot, I look hot and tanned. I am smiling. My breasts show rounded under my shirt. This will be a sexy picture. Cate will like this, I think. I have never felt this way about my body before—recognizing it as desirable. It is the same body I have always had, but I am different in it now.

The last stop my mother and I make is in Kayenta, Arizona. As we drive there, night is coming on and the clouds above us turn slowly from pink to peach to gold. The clouds are so close and the color so intense that I feel as if we are rising up into them, as if we are flying, as if at any moment we will burst through this blanket of gold and be soaring among stars in a blue-black sky. At the hotel we have Navajo fry bread and salad for dinner. Just to watch her order from a menu, to see her make a choice about what it is that she wants, such a simple choice, gives me a feeling of great intimacy. Neither one of us sleeps well. Clearly, we don't want to go home.

As we drive through Monument Valley the next morning, the sun comes up deep burnt-orange behind the weird sandstone sculptures of the valley. My mother keeps saying to me that this is the best vacation she has ever had. "You're easy to be with," she says. She is surprised by the things I do for her, such as open doors and carry her suitcase. "You are so polite," she says.

When we get back to Salt Lake she wants to have our pictures developed right away. We drop them off at the camera counter at Safeway, even before we reach home, and rush back to get them exactly an hour later. We show them to my father. He looks at three or four and puts the stack aside.

∽

There is another picture of me fly fishing. I am older still. Maybe thirty. I stand in a wide, curving stream with my fly rod, casting out into the silver water with trees rising behind me and gray-blue mountains beyond that. The picture looks romantic and perfect: girl and stream. Mountains. Fish. But I remember this time. I remember my heavy pack, the black flies biting at my neck, my Royal Humpy caught on the rocks and willows behind me. I remember not catching fish and wondering again why I was out there in the stream up to my thighs in water.

I remember, too, that there was then, and has been every time I have gone fishing with my father, a laughing in the water and the pleasant crunch of gravel under my boots and relief offered by the cool wafts of watery air that came up from the stream. There was the rich smell of fish and weeds and pebbles and muck from the undercut banks hung over with grass.

I remember, too, amid the peace and the real joy, a feeling of being trapped. I don't love this, I wanted to shout out so that my voice echoed off the mountains. I'll never love it like you do. Can't you see? I'm doing it for you, to be with you. I'm trying. And it isn't working.

My father agrees to take me to the train station at five in the morning, long before my train is supposed to leave. Already he has been up for hours, typing on his computer at the breakfast table. He will go straight from the train station to his lab and work. He asks me if I will come and visit him at his cabin in Montana this summer. I tell him no. I can't spend time with him alone now, until something, anything, even something small, changes between us. He asks me what I would like for my graduation present and suggests some stocks that his parents gave him when he graduated with his Ph.D. in biology. In the secret, angry language that passes between us, I hear him saying that he loves me. I want him to say it out loud. I want him, out loud, to ask me something real about my life and to tell me something real about his.

Our strongest connection lies in fly fishing, but I want more than this—I want him to understand me in my wholeness. I want him to know what else there is about me besides Fishergirl. "You want me to fish with you," I want to say, "I want you to see who I am." And I want to tell him this, that I am an ordinary woman who is thirty-four-years old and owns a stained, smelly fishing vest, only half of the pockets with anything in them at all. I am an ordinary woman with a crumpled and eclectic collection of flies, an unused fly-tying kit, two fly rods, two reels, some cracked nylon wading shoes, a pair of old-fashioned rubber waders and a couple of books on fly tying. And besides all of this, I have two cats. I like to drink strong coffee in the morning. I dance the two-step to country music. I own a leather miniskirt and purple cowboy boots. I love my crewcut hair. I sip chamomile tea every night before bed. I have gone canoeing in the wilderness alone. I won a medal in a cross-country ski race. I have ordinary desires, to love and be loved in return. Bills to pay. I am moving to Alaska. And I am a lesbian. He has no idea of who I am.

He hugs me awkwardly, and when I look at him tears are pooling in his eyes. After he leaves I sit in the waiting area and open *The River Why* again. In the last chapters, Gus goes off to a cabin in the woods to fish and be alone, released finally from the pressing of both of his strong-willed parents—the fly fisher and the bait angler, Gus finds himself, and he finds his true love, a glimmering fishing girl with apple blossoms in her hair. In many ways he gives up on his family, gives up about them ever being different, and sets off to have a new life.

One day, upon returning to his cabin, Gus sees, by the stream that runs in front of his house, an old man with a straw hat tipped over one eye, lounging in a chair and fishing with worms. He doesn't recognize the fellow and lets him be. Farther along the stream Gus sees an old woman elegantly decked out in tweeds, fly casting, perfectly. He doesn't recognize her either, but watches her for a while, impressed. Soon he begins to realize that he does know these two. He realizes that they are his mother and father and that they have changed.

When the train arrives I shut my book and move out into the darkness of the platform. I shove my bags aboard and settle into my seat, my face pressed against the window. The train doesn't move for a long time, and I drift off to sleep, dreaming. In the dream my mother is in her kitchen. She wants me to spend more time with my father. "He has something important to show you," she says. My father enters the kitchen, pale and thin, with red and tired eyes, but he is excited, like a boy, showing me his latest miraculous inventions—a new way to fasten rain gutters to the cabin roof, or this, a clip for attaching a cable to a battery, or this, blueprints for a straw toolshed. As I turn away from him, he collapses, folding to the floor like a dropped cloth, and I run to him calling "Daddy, Daddy, Daddy."

I am startled awake by the train lurching away from the platform with a deep metallic creak and a moan. My heart is pumping unevenly in my chest. I whisper to myself, the words coming out softly and making misty spots on the window glass near my face, "Is it time?" Is it all right to go ahead and admit that I am blood of his blood, that I am my father's daughter, that *this*, that loving to fish, is a gift, that we love some of the same things? In a moment so bright and quick that I hardly know what it is, I understand one thing—no one can really do that to anyone else; no one can really fix or freeze anyone else. But it has been hard to contradict the molding. The more I know who I am, the more I will be able to see who I am, I think, smiling to myself over how much of a riddle it sounds. I am, at least partly, and all on my own, Fishergirl.

As we begin to move, to gather speed, something begins to gather in me—it comes slowly, then faster, then comes on all at once, like a river of heat rolling up from my toes, filling the hollowness of my body, making my scalp prickle, my fingers tremble. This is joy, this thing I was so unaccustomed to not so long ago. *I have changed.* I close my eyes and see a glimmering girl emerge from a silver trout, lithe and shining, running, calling me by my name.

OWL AT NIGHT,

OWL IN THE MORNING

I T WAS SPRING and Craig and I were on our way back to St. Paul from Lake Bemidji, where we had spent the opening weekend of Minnesota fishing season. We stopped, as we tended to do, at a park on the way home. We were wanting desperately to stay away from the city one last night. When we did this we would arise the next day well before dawn and hurtle back to our jobs and classes, sometimes having only enough time for a shower and to throw on fresh clothes before we had to be at appointed real-life destinations, dirt from the weekend still under our nails.

This May night was moist, but it was a spring wetness that stayed outside your bones. The night was fresh with green shadows and the sound of leftover raindrops falling from trees. We made venison steaks on our tiny grill and pasta on the Coleman stove. I uncorked a bottle of red wine. After dinner we each had a steaming mug of tea and we walked over to the Crow Wing River in the dark. We had heard sounds, the sounds of migrating Canada geese returning to Minnesota for the summer. They were soft noises, the noises of sleepy geese laying themselves down. We stood by the side of the river whispering, "Where are they?" We could only make out dark shapes on an island in the river channel.

We stood quietly, reaching out for sound. We heard water. We heard, I swear, dirt being pushed skyward by plants coming up from the earth. We heard the first important, quiet sounds of spring.

Then clearly, loudly, so loud I jumped and spilled my tea, came the sound of an owl behind us in the pines. *Who who who-whooo. Who who who-whooo.* We turned and saw it vaguely, huge and brown, its great feathery ears poking up and its eyes gleaming in the faded light. We could have touched it, it was so close. Not long after the three of us met eyes, the owl, with a heavy *whoomp* of wing, lifted its body and sailed away into the night woods.

Craig would tease me forever after this, as I tried to imitate the sound of that owl, forcing air through my puffed-out cheeks, *Who who who whooo-whooo.*

It was fall and we had gone to Roseau, up near Canada, to hunt ducks with friends on a canal that runs as a border water between the two countries. Late at night we were still up, finishing venison chili and standing around a big fire.

The sky lit up with colors I had never seen. I was convinced Craig and the others were joking with me, that this had to be a carnival in some nearby town, or a fire. I had never seen such brilliant northern lights and could not believe they were real. The sky was moving, dancing, swimming. The sky was a school of many-colored fish. The sky was full of the glowing bodies of angels. The sky was pink and red and green and blue and yellow and white. It went on and on and on. Someone tried to answer my questions of why, how does that work, with talk about particles or ions.

The next morning before it was light we were up, cracking through the canal, the thin ice tinkling against the metal bow of our canoe. It was slow going. Finally we stopped on one side of a small beaver dam, while the others went over and beyond. We pulled the canoe up onto the snowy bank and covered it with a piece of burlap for camouflage, and we waited. We were waiting for that first flight of fat, sleek, emerald-headed northern mallards to come sailing down the canal.

Around us was short frozen grass and brush and tamarack. Just as the sun was coming up, when everything began to flicker and shine with the snow and the light, all the ice and grass and whiteness and clearness becoming like a blazing light in the cold, just then, when there was not another place I could ever imagine being more happy, across the canal, in the dark green of the forest on the other side, another owl hooted out a clear morning song. *Who who whooooo.* The notes hung in the cold air and then dissipated, like snow dissolving in warm air before it can touch the ground.

After Craig and I stopped hunting together, after we were no longer married, he came back from a fall deer-hunting trip he had taken with a friend, and told me about a third owl, an owl he heard on that trip, about how it had startled him in his deer stand, and I knew that this meant that he remembered the other owls—the night owl on the Crow Wing River and the morning owl on the Canadian border. I knew this meant he would, forever, like me, remember those other owls, and that he was sad too.

BASIC LIFESAVING

P EOPLE WHO WANT to kill themselves will try again and again until they are successful," my mother told me, repeating what the doctor had told her after Ally had tried for the next-to-last time to kill herself. *That* time she swallowed a bottle of aspirin and sliced her skin with a razor as she lay in a hot bath. She did keep trying, it was true. The final time, Ally swallowed a lethal dose of anti-depressants. "If a person really wants to kill herself," my mother said, "there's nothing you can do."

The meaning of what my mother said is clear to me. There was no practical way for us to stop Ally from swallowing pills, from slitting her wrists; no practical way for anyone to watch over my sister twenty-four hours a day, follow her to the bathroom, wait while she showered, ride with her in her Volkswagen Bug to her job at the bookstore, lie down with her when she took a nap in the afternoon, accompany her on her daily jogs. I understand that there are some things that we cannot control, other people being one of them; someone else's will to live being one of them. You cannot save someone who does not want to be saved.

For all its truth, however, there is something deeply false about this too; something false and apathetic about there being nothing you can do to help a person in such trouble. *There is nothing you can do* . . . is an excuse to watch and wait, wringing your hands, hoping for the best while someone you love spirals downward. *There is nothing you can do* . . . is some kind of armor against your own helplessness, some kind of corrupted prayer that at least keeps *you* safe in the face of that perverted instinct of suicide. It is some kind of giving up human hope to fate and chance. *There is nothing you can do* ... provides some kind of comfortable tradition for inaction—that's what the doctor said, we tell each other, *there's nothing we could have done.*

We risk enormously, we risk our hearts, maybe even our own lives, when we *do* something, when we face the fear that our efforts may be useless, utterly, against the force of someone's wish to die. We risk becoming intimate with the horror that is making our sister or brother or friend want to die. Who wouldn't want to turn their back on that, on something so horrible, on something as horrible as death overcoming? But it seems to me now, in cases like this, in the case of suicide, any gesture toward life, however eventually ineffective, is the bare rock foundation of love.

No matter what you do to try to stop them ...

On the canoe trip Sam cried a lot. She started crying when she saw the first dead cat on the freeway leading out of St. Paul. Later she would see deer and ducks and more cats and a dog, squashed flat or partly mangled, a splatter of their blood, their feathers, their fur, marking the center of the highway. She cried all the way to where we stopped the car and hoisted the canoes to the ground.

It was the end of May in northern Wisconsin and Sam and I were traveling with two other friends, Janet and Hutch, down the Namekagon River, from the town of Trego to the St. Croix River. It was a trip in celebration of spring, masterminded by Janet and Hutch years before, and repeated at the end of each long Minnesota winter. Sam and I had been invited that year partly because two of the regular canoeists had other engagements.

Sam and I had met each other and become lovers only a few months before, and I had already sensed some restless, angry sadness in her. I had no idea of the origin at first, and it brought out in me all my saving instincts. The canoe trip, I thought, would be a nice break for the both of us, a nice break for her.

It started raining as I waited with the canoes at the put-in point while

Janet and Sam drove a car around to the place we would take the canoes out in three days' time. It started raining then, and for three days it rained off and on, pouring and misting, always wet. Only at the end of the trip, as we sailed down into the bigger and faster and wider St. Croix, did the sun boldly come out and a dry wind come up.

The whole time, Sam hated the rain, and she hated the wood ticks too. The wood ticks on this trip were worse than any of us ever remembered. They dropped onto our necks from tree branches and crawled up our legs from the grass. There was no way, it seemed, to avoid them; we paid close attention to slight stirrings on our skin, under our sweaters and rain gear, and searched behind each other's ears.

We started the trip as three women in two canoes. Hutch had been held up by work and would meet us several hours down-river. Sam took my big brown Grumman, loaded with full coolers of ice, pop, beer, juice and fresh fruit. She would try it by herself for a while, she said gamely, and she hopped in and dipped the paddle and the current took her and off we went.

Janet and I quickly got ahead of her, but kept looking back over our shoulders, keeping track. When we saw the bow of her canoe emerge from around the bend of a bank, and saw that she was all right, we waved and she waved back and we carried on ahead. It took me hours to realize she was in trouble. Later, after we stopped and switched places, we found out that Sam had spent the morning and afternoon bouncing off first one bank then another, like a wild billiard ball. It just so happened that when we saw her for those brief glimpses, she was on a straight path.

"We need to stop," I yelled forward to Janet, when I saw that Sam had a scared, tired look on her face and that she wasn't in control of the canoe at all.

"Not here," she said. "There's nowhere to pull up."

The banks were high and the water was deep and fast, but I couldn't see any place any safer up ahead, so I insisted, and I steered us to the left bank and dug my paddle in hard and swung us around so the bow was pointing up-river and we paddled hard until Janet could grab onto a thick willow bough. Sam managed to reach us and we grabbed the gunnel of her canoe and rested in the water, while I made Sam switch with me right there. We stayed low and didn't rock the canoe too much, but it was scary and it made me think what I would do if one of us toppled over into the fast-moving river.

All of my siblings and I had taken Basic Lifesaving. Ally and Ed had gone on to be lifeguards in the summers. I had never had to save anyone from drowning, but I had memorized the routine. First, don't go in after them. Throw the drowning person a line or lie on your stomach and hand them a pole or a towel. Second, if you have to go in after them and they struggle with you, push them away or dive deeper and they might let go. I remember a film of someone actually punching a guy in the face to knock him out so that he could be dragged to safety. Third, if the person is cooperative, or unconscious, grab their chin with your hand, or drape one arm across their chest and sidestroke your way to safety. Sometimes, I remembered from the classes and films, there were some people you just couldn't save—the ones who panicked, the ones who tried to take you down with them. You had to just let them drown.

"Be careful," Janet kept saying to me. "Watch out." After Sam got settled in the other canoe with Janet, I stood up and braced myself against the gunnel and the yoke and hauled a cooler and some other gear out of Janet and Sam's canoe and loaded it into the bow of mine, so the weight was mostly in the front. That had been one of Sam's problems—the weight in the canoe was all at the back, so the bow kept riding high and getting swept around in the current. When all this was done, we pushed off again into the current and went on to meet up with Hutch and find our first campsite.

The next morning it was still raining. The tent floor was damp. Sam and I lay in the tent together watching the beaver across the river build his house and collect his dinner. Back and forth he went, his heavy head above the water, making a hard "V" of a wake, dragging branches three or four times his size from the bank into the river. We thought we could hear the beaver chomping away in the woods. We thought we could even hear the small trees fall. As we watched, we saw flashes of orange and red in the woods—scarlet tanagers and orioles. Nothing was quite itself yet in these spring woods—the sounds were softer and the green was not yet the hard green of mid- or late summer.

Sam got up and fiddled around under the tarp we had strung over our upturned canoes, which served as our kitchen. I heard the stove hiss and in about fifteen minutes Sam brought me a hot cup of coffee with cream in it. She brought it to the tent door and took the sopping wet flap back and handed the coffee in, and then later she brought a bowl of hot water and a bottle of peppermint soap and a washcloth. I came out of the tent naked and stood in the wet grass, mist coming down around me, and bathed.

After a lazy morning, Sam and I headed off to collect firewood. We'd need a lot, since we'd decided not to switch camps that day, but to stay put because of the rain. We hauled great sodden logs out of the woods, sawed them apart with Janet's handsaw, then propped them against one another in a tepee over the fire to dry. As we were breaking and stacking wood, suddenly Sam stepped away and flung a stick into the river, hard, with all her grit and muscle. The stick zinged its way through the trees, snapping off new leaves, and landed with a loud splash. I looked at her quizzically. "Why did you do that?" Her face was pale, her dark brown eyes stony. Standing there she was like barbed wire, stretched so tight that it would twang if you plucked it. "I had a dog," she said, "I *have* a dog. Back in Montana." She picked up another stick and struck the ground beside her, again and again, then flung that stick too, into the river. She threw it far, with the ease of an athlete and the power of someone who wanted to hurt something.

When I'd met Sam she'd said that she'd moved to Minnesota from Montana, where she'd been a high-school history teacher, to go to graduate school at the University of Minnesota. She had relatives in Minnesota, she said. It was a natural choice. But I found out later that she'd also moved to be with a woman she loved, and that the woman had unceremoniously dumped her immediately after her arrival, Sam's belongings still tightly packed in the back of a U-Haul truck.

I heard a lot from Sam about how great Montana was. That was where she was moving back to, soon, she said. That was where she and this other woman had fallen in love, and out of love, and in again, and had spent nights together in the back of Sam's pickup, listening to the rain fall on the camper top. It had been two years and Sam still froze in her tracks and her heart raced whenever she saw this woman by accident at a concert or in line at the grocery store or across a lawn on campus.

That afternoon on the Namekagon Janet and Hutch and Sam and I sat around our smoky fire, drying the wet wood and drinking tea or whiskey and hot water, our hands wrapped around our mugs. We told stories and read to each other until we got bored with that and then we went for walks.

Sam and I made our way through the wet woods, pulling back branches that sent showers of water down upon us, fingering small flowers that glowed in the shadowless rain light. We made a funny pair—Sam all tall and lean and leggy, draped in a black oiled poncho and a wide-brimmed black cowboy hat, and me, short, stocky, dressed up in my bright-blue rain jacket and pants, a Minnesota Twins baseball cap pulled down tight on my head.

We finally sat down on a hill, among some pines, overlooking the river. The pines had dropped so many needles onto the forest floor that what we sat on was cushioned and soft, like a bed. Sam sat next to me on the hill and leaned against me. Her body was hard and heavy, dense and muscular from running and biking. The hair poking out from under her hat lay in wet dark-brown curls on her long neck.

I realized, after some time, that she was crying again. I put my arm around her and pulled her close. Our legs dangled over the side of the bluff. There was soft rain landing all around and the river in front of us, brown and fast, and slight spring green all around. She was afraid, she said, her shoulders shaking against my chest. In her voice there was an edgy hopelessness. Her crying was shallow and painful, like breaths drawn into a bruised chest. "Sometimes," she said, "I think about killing myself." She didn't know what to do, she said. She didn't know what was wrong with her. Tears made little rivulets down her cheeks. She wiped them and they became dirty tracks.

"There are no ticks in Montana," she told me. And no mosquitoes. And there was *always* sunshine. And mountains. And she had *friends* there. And there was never anything like this droopy wetness. "This place sucks," she said, as if she'd made up her mind then, finally, to leave it, to go back out west. But then she'd turn right around and think up ten reasons to stay. How was she supposed to make up her mind? How was she to know the right thing to do?

I didn't tell her what I thought, that this pain of hers was only partly about landscape, and the rest of it was about having a broken heart, and because of that her grief would follow her anywhere she went. What I told her instead was this: that it was all right to be sad, that it wouldn't last forever, and that I had been there once and I had come back around and I was glad of it. "You're a good person," I said. "Everything will be all right. You'll find the right thing to do. Everything will be all right."

. . . they'll find a way to do it.

What we did:

My parents made sure that Ally received therapy, after she first tried to slice her wrist open with a hunting knife of mine. We knew, I knew, it was the right thing, the only thing, to do, to put her in the care of professionals. She would be fine. But then, even after she promised her doctor she wouldn't do it again, she did it again, and again and again. And she did it finally with medication her psychiatrist had prescribed.

My mother made sure whenever Ally called her, usually in tears, that she spent time with my sister on the phone. It was something she could do. But, my mother said, she got to feeling burdened by those phone calls and would sometimes want to hang up when she heard Ally's on-the-edge-of-crying voice on the other end of the line, "Hi Mom . . . It's me. . . ."

One minute Ally would be happy and normal, ice skating around and around a festively lit downtown ice rink, and then she'd burst into tears when you said it was time to go. One minute she'd be happy and normal and the next she'd be taking her boyfriend to the hospital for six stitches because in a rage she'd smashed a jar of peanut butter over his head. He would tell my mother that Ally had gotten angry because he'd grabbed her wrist and shaken her fist open and what fell out was a handful of pills she had been about to swallow. My mother told him he'd done the right thing to stop her.

The least I could do was be sympathetic and encouraging. But when she started blaming things on the rest of us, that was the end of the line for me. What was wrong with her anyway? I stopped listening. It just made me sad. Nothing I said made her any happier. Fed up with her, finally, I wrote a letter to my mother a few months before Ally died.

Please do not discuss this with Ally. I got a very depressing note from her today. I told my mother that Ally blamed her, blamed her drinking, for the problems she was having. I thought that was funny, I said. From my perspective it was the therapy that was doing Ally harm—all that intro- spection, all that looking for bad things in her past. I offered this solu- tion: *What she needs is to be put in a place where someone else's life, or her own life for that matter, depends on her—where she is put face to face with the reality of life and death, with really surviving. Then she'll see how it is . . .*

If some person wants to kill herself . . .

Earlier that spring, before the canoe trip, Sam and I had driven to Stockholm, Wisconsin to stay overnight in the Merchant's Inn, an old rooming house above an antique store, across the street from a store that sold Amish quilts. On that spring day we took coffee and a loaf of lemon bread from the Jenny Lind Bakery next door and walked. We took the warm dirt road as far as where it turned sharply to the right, then we cut off across a field, making our way toward the bluff overlooking Lake Pepin and the Mississippi River. The ground was moist and the rich fur- rows we walked over sank a bit beneath our feet.

Far ahead we saw deer among the bent and dried corn stalks and when they sensed us, the deer rose up and sailed, graceful as fish, into the woods. Sam looked at me, as if on a dare, and began to run. I chased her and we ran in circles, pretending we were deer. When we got to the edge of the bluff we sat in the hot grass and ripped off hunks of bread and passed the thermos of coffee back and forth. "What a miracle it is that spring comes every year," I said to her. "It's not the same spring, but every year it comes, some version of it, after winter."

A few hours later, on the way back to the Merchant's Inn, we went directly through the thick woods, down the bluff, instead of around on the road. We stopped to look closely at bloodroot and new violets and marsh marigolds that were coming up bravely through the thick forest grass. I spotted the metal tip of an arrow, driven deep into a log; a hunter's shot that missed. Sam stopped ahead of me and turned around and, mo- tioning to the woods, to the sunshine, and to me too, said, "Gret, this is what's real. This is what's real and the other stuff is just a cover." We found a baseball near the side of the road on our way back to town and we played catch in the sun. "You," she said, smiling. "You have a good arm!"

On the way back to the Twin Cities from that trip to Stockholm, we passed a red-brown beaver, flat beside the road. He had obviously been on his way from the woods to the small stream on the other side of the road and had gotten hit by a car. Sam drove on for a mile or so past the beaver, then abruptly pulled over and made a U-turn. Something turned over in her, quickly, from the giddy joy of the morning to this. Looking at me hard she said, "I don't care if you think I'm nuts, I'm going back for that beaver."

We pulled up behind the beaver on the side of the road. Sam asked me what we should do. I told her to get gloves from the back of the car and we'd pick it up and move it. "Where to?" she asked. "To the water. That's what it would want," I said, feeling as if I had to make no sudden moves, as if I were handling explosives.

The beaver was flat against the warm pavement, all four feet splayed, the thick webs between its toes still soft. Blood trickled from the corner of its mouth. We picked it up, its flat, fleshy-scaly tail falling as we lifted it, and we carefully stepped down the grassy bank to the stream. Sam picked a handful of small violets and laid them on the beaver's back, petted the thick fur, caressed the webbed feet, and wept. Then we set the beaver body adrift in the stream, pushing it out into the current with a long willow branch. As we drove away we watched from the car as the beaver floated down the stream beside us, bobbing around eddies and under fallen tree branches, the violets riding on its back.

Soon after that, on the same stretch of road, we came upon the turtles: two dozen of them at least, some flattened, their shells no protection against the weight of a car, some partly maimed, their guts or a smashed foot trailing behind them as they tried to make their way to the other side of the road. We stopped again, and Sam got out to aid those still in the middle of the highway. I pointed and she looked over her shoulder to see, up the road and down the road, more turtles, stupidly making their slow way across the blacktop, and more just inching their stretched out necks over the grass on the swamp side of the road.

"There were too many to help," Sam said as we drove away. She was crying still. Her shirt front was wet. "But we did something."

... what can you do?

We sat on the banks of the Namekagon. Sam was crying. I held her. I listened to her tell me a story, the story of a horse. The horse belonged to a friend of hers in Montana. It was a terrific horse. Sam was out riding one day on this horse. It was the first time Sam had ridden it and she was out alone. She was riding with her big black hat on and cowboy boots and jeans, her long legs down the side of the horse's body, and she had on a long slicker, and she and the horse went down into a streambed and the horse sank. It was quicksand.

Sam jumped off and pulled the saddle off and then there was nothing else she could do. She stood on the bank of the streambed and called encouragement to the horse and prayed. The horse was up to its shoulders in the quicksand and struggling, sinking, snorting wildly. Then all of a sudden, Sam said, it collected all of itself. She could see the muscles tighten, the eyes harden. And with one great, violent heave, the horse exploded out of the quicksand and onto the bank and stood there and shook and shivered. Despite its great courage, the horse later died, inexplicably, from something that had nothing to do with the quicksand.

They'll try again and again ...

I told a friend of mine that the idea of being happy appealed to me. She said that it appealed to her too, but she thought it might not be possible to be happy all the time, and perhaps it was not even the best goal. Rather than being happy all the time, she said, she might strive instead to *feel* all the time, to be alive all the time. That's a lot, she said, not needing to anesthetize feeling with all of our culture's ready anesthetics, not to mention what she called all of our personal psychological hiding places.

It's nothing to take lightly, another friend said, this business of feeling things. Those who never learned that delicate and complex system of translating bodily feeling into meaning are at risk for two things: overdoing it on the anesthetizing devices and springing a screw and losing control. And this is no joke, my friend said. When you depend on those anesthetizing devices and then for some reason they are suddenly unavailable, the shear power of your own emotions can overwhelm you. "Think about it," she said. "Your *own* emotions can *kill* you."

We know our minds, another friend said, by listening to our bodies first. We know our minds by paying attention to the way our blood courses, the way our shoulders bunch and gnaw, the way our stomachs knot, the way our finger joints ring with pain. We know fear and trust and tenderness and shame, all of them, in our bodies first. When we don't pay attention to our bodies, we can't know our minds, she said. And when we don't know our own minds, we accidentally, all the time, hurt people we love, including ourselves.

Learning how to feel seems an awkward and embarrassing enterprise, especially on the cusp of the twenty-first century, when so much intellectual labor has gone into dismantling the very notion that we have bodies at all—real material bodies—much less that we have feelings that are grounded in bodily experience. How do you learn to interpret the language of the body? How do you learn the habit of attention that is necessary to feel? Would there were courses: Basic Lifesaving—a course in techniques for keeping oneself alive. First, this is what a feeling is—this is anger, this is joy, this is sadness. Second, sadness is not the same as despair. Third, here is how to keep from hurting yourself. Here is how to keep from hurting someone you love. Here is how to keep from scaring yourself to death.

. . . and again, until they are dead.

When I first met Sam she told me a story, in the way that people who meet and like each other tell each other significant stories about their lives, stories that will reveal some fundamental thing about themselves that they want the other person to be aware of. Once, Sam said, she ran over one of her own cats.

She was at her lover's house getting ready to drive home. Her kitten had been playing under the car, so Sam looked for the kitten to make sure it wasn't under the car anymore. Not seeing the kitten, Sam got into her truck and started it up and drove down the alley and then heard the sound of a little bell tinkling. She got out of the truck and looked back and her cat was flopping on the asphalt in spasms.

Sam's lover then was a hunter. Sam rushed into the house calling out for her lover to get a shotgun and come out and shoot the cat. By the time the two of them got outside with the loaded gun the kitten was dead. Sam punched her fists into the metal garbage cans in the alley until her hands bled.

She was like something without a skin, Sam was. Nothing to protect her at all against the occasional awfulness of everyday life.

"I found a dead duck," Sam called and said to me one day. "I want you to come over and help me figure out what to do." She had been running at Lake of the Isles and the duck had been there by the side of the path and she had picked it up and taken it home. We agreed the best thing to do was to skin the duck and send the feathery hide to her friend who tied fishing flies in Montana, then feed what good breast meat there was to her three cats, and then bury the rest.

With my sharpened fillet knife, I slit along the duck's belly just under the skin and cut around the beak and then I started to peel the skin away from the head and neck and away from the breast. When I was done, I had on the cutting board the ugliest dark-red cadaver—all meat, no skin. I cut away a good portion of the duck's breast and we boiled it for the cats. Sam then took the carcass away from me. She had dug a grave in the backyard garden, and she was taking the duck there to bury it.

After cleaning up in the kitchen I went out into Sam's living room and found that she had not gone out to the garden, but that she was sitting on the couch cradling the dead duck in her arms, like a child or a doll, rocking it, listening to a particular song on the radio, and crying.

Another time, I was helping Sam train for the Twin Cities Marathon. We were out in the country and I drove on ahead of her in the car with a map, water, and dry socks, plotting a route that would be exactly half the length of the marathon. I came upon a dead raccoon. I stopped the car, looked back down the road to make sure that Sam had not seen me, jogged across the road, picked up the heavy gray and black thing by its front paws and was dragging it off into the weeds, its back feet leaving a scuffed trail on the dirt road, when Sam loomed up over the rise. I thought I was doing something to help her, something to protect her from the mess and gore, but she saw the dead raccoon anyway, and me trying to hide it from her.

When someone wants to kill herself badly enough . . .

This is the story of how I saved my own life.

I had been out . . .

No, let me back up. I had left my husband. I was all alone . . .

Let me start over.

I had left my husband and I thought I would never be alone. At first I was distracted from my own fear by kind phone calls and visits from friends. Then the phone calls stopped, as they had to. No one had time to care for me in that way, every hour of every day.

It was then that my own fear rose up. I had once and for all taken full responsibility for my own life, and I realized a truth that came over me in a nauseating wave—that I was in this alone. It was, after all, *my* life, not anyone else's. I had left my husband. I had leapt. It wasn't the *reasons* for the leap that scared me. It was the actual *leaping*. I was still falling, wind rushing by my face. At night I lay in bed, curled under a single sheet, dressed in a T-shirt and underwear, and my heart beat wildly. I felt sick to my stomach and I cried. Night after night. I couldn't believe what I had done.

One night I had gone out with friends to cheer myself up. I was miserable. I spooned my after-theater cheesecake into my dry mouth with a heavy hand. I drank too many glasses of wine. I was stubbornly silent, wanting them to ask, "What's the matter?" I became unaccountably embarrassed, wanted to die, when someone said that no, it wasn't Strindberg who wrote *A Doll's House*, it was Ibsen. How could I have been so stupid? What kind of a worthless English graduate student was I anyway?

On my way home, in the compact darkness of my car, on the freeway between Minneapolis and St. Paul, I decided that I would kill myself. It was as if the idea came on cue; a post-hypnotic suggestion.

I parked my car in the street, as usual, went up the well-lit stairs, let myself into my apartment, set my wallet and keys on the top of the filing cabinet next to my desk, as usual, and walked directly to the kitchen sink. I reached to my right and opened the silverware drawer and took out my best knife, from the set of Chicago Cutlery Craig and I got for our wedding.

I held my wrist, tender inside up, over the stainless-steel sink, and with my right hand I pressed the sharp blade of the knife into my wrist, all white and blue-veined. I pressed hard. I didn't want to carve, to slice; I wanted to press. I kept pressing. I had stopped crying. A welt started to form on my wrist. I knew if I moved the knife at all it would slice me open.

I saw it happen. I saw it played out before me like some terrible film—the white walls of the kitchen spattered with red, me stumbling to bed, wrapping myself in the white sheets, the sheets turning red, me bleeding to death in bed, someone finding me, the mattress soaked with my blood.

I watched myself die. And the horror of it stopped me. I felt sorry for myself. I felt such tenderness for my own self that I stopped. I dropped the knife into the sink. Then, knowing I would not want to be reminded of this in the morning, I made sure there was no blood on the blade and put the knife neatly back in the silverware drawer.

I went to bed and curled up, sobbing, twisted in my sheets. Bubbly spit ran out the sides of my mouth. In the dark I raised my right fist above my head and I pulled it down into my face. I raised my hand again, and again drove my fist down into my face. My cat leapt away. Each time I heard that strangely satisfying sound, the sound of my own fist meeting the soft skin of my face, my fist meeting with my cheekbone, I cried out. When I awoke my face was swollen on the right side and cut and black and blue. I stared at my reflection in the mirror for a long time. I watched my own fingers touch the bruises, trace the cuts. "Who did this to you?" I asked myself in the mirror.

I wore sunglasses for a week when I could, and when I couldn't, I told people I had walked into a door in the dark. Some of them didn't say anything. Some of them raised their eyebrows, letting me know that was an old story, about the door and the dark. Some of them thought that Craig had hit me. The truth was, this had always been a protection for me; no one could ever hurt me more than I could hurt myself. No one had ever beaten me like I beat myself.

. . . it's only a matter of how and when, not if.

Not long after I'd thought about killing myself, I went to a doctor with the idea that I might have some tests done to see if I had damaged my health yet, by smoking for thirteen years. If I wasn't yet beyond repair, I would quit.

In one test I had to blow into a hollow plastic tube and my breath pushed a little red arrow up at the other end of the tube, rather like those attractions at the fair where you hit a spot with a hammer and a ball flies up and hits a bell. In another test, I blew through a tube connected to a mechanical birthday cake. My job was to suck in as much air as possible and then force it out as fast and as long as possible, as if I were blowing the candles out. Then I had a chest X-ray. The doctor also listened to my breathing with a stethoscope.

When I went back to the doctor to get my results she said I was fine. "Fine." That was all she said. I wanted a copy of the results. "A copy?" she said. She showed me the tiny graphs from the breath tests. "The graph actually shows a borderline obstruction," she said, pointing with her pencil. "You can take air in but you can't blow it out as well."

"How was the X-ray?" I asked.

"Fine," she said.

"What did you see on it?" I asked.

She pointed toward a blank light screen on the wall, as if it held my X-ray in it and said, "Well . . ."

"No," I said, "I mean I want to see it. That's why I had it done."

So I went down to X-ray and I saw it. The technician, acting as if he were indulging a child, clipped the picture of my lungs to the light board and flicked the switch, and there, in hues of gray and black, was my body from the waist up. How beautiful it all was. There I was, see-through, my collarbone, the bones of my arms hanging down, my spine, my heart tucked there behind my sternum, and my ribs and my diaphragm and my lungs. I had clean lungs, no white patches. And the filmy bits of bronchia and veins fanned out across my lungs like small rivers and their tiny tributaries. I was still all right. I hadn't yet done myself irreparable harm.

We sat on the banks of the Namekagon and I held Sam in the rain, and all I could think of to do was say to her "Of course you are afraid. There's nothing to be more afraid of." Over and over I told her the same things: "You are a good person, I love you, everything will be fine, the world is a miraculous place, you are a good person, everything will be fine, I love you, everything will be fine, the world is a miraculous place, I love you, you are a good person, the world . . ."

BLUEBERRIES

B LUEBERRIES ARE THE FRUIT of the woods that mark high late sum
mer, the best last days of July and the early days of August. These
are berry days; days when all the trees are at their greenest; days when
the air is dense and humid, when you walk about in shorts and bare feet
hardly believing, hardly remembering, that you own wool jackets and
down parkas that protect you from the cold that is only months away; days
when you have only the vaguest memory of chill dry air, of colored leaves,
of what will come next—hunting for grouse and ducks and geese, then deer,
and fishing through the ice; days when ice is inconceivable, unless it comes
in a glass of lemonade. These are the nights of frogs and raccoons and
nighthawks; nights full of moons and stars, of thunderstorms that frighten
and thrill and bring lightning and torrents of rain.

This year I pick blueberries in the piney, sandy woods off Big Bay on
Madeline Island, with Craig and his daughters. The island and the bay
are a ferry ride away from Bayfield, Wisconsin, on the south shore of Lake
Superior. Craig and I no longer live in the same house, but we still do
some things together, like picking blueberries.

Blueberry picking forces you to be meticulous. Each berry needs to
be picked separately. Sometimes, if you are lucky, you get to take a blue
cluster of three or four, but usually each tiny wild berry must be picked
by itself. And so, every berry counts.

Sometimes I eat the berries as I pick, but mostly I concentrate on filling my gallon pail. Every berry counts, I think, as I walk through the woods, looking downward, looking for the tiny pointed leaves of the blueberry bushes, looking for the roundest, biggest, bluest orbs. Don't skip that one, bend over, pick it up, every berry counts, I tell myself. I am thinking of blueberry pies, of blueberry pancakes, of blueberry syrup and blueberry muffins.

There is nothing that matches these small berries, so densely purple when baked into a pie. Perhaps it is my imagination, but I think that I can smell them in the woods when they are near, the same way I think I can pick up the barky, buttery scent of morel mushrooms in the woods in the spring. The blueberries smell of freshness, of summer, of purple juiciness.

Blueberry picking is absorbing. As I pick I think of a story I heard about a woman getting lost blueberry picking, and being found the next day, having eaten all her berries, which was all she had to eat. Could it happen to me? I wonder, as I wander off, only occasionally looking up to see Craig or one of the girls, to mark my place in the woods. Sometimes I call out to them. Sometimes we come together by accident, wandering in the same direction, and compare the blueberries in our pails. Craig's is empty this time and he jokes with me that he spilled it, but I think he has brought two pots. Either that or he has emptied an already full pail into the crown of his straw hat and has hidden it under a nearby pine.

I hum to myself as I meander about and I think of the lady with the long blonde hair who came to us by invitation the night before and sat around our campfire and told us something we already knew, all of us. She told us that peace of mind is the most important thing.

She was our neighbor in the camp next to ours. She had seen us trying to start a fire with wet wood and wet paper. It had rained the night before. We saw her watching us and paid her little mind, passing her off as nosey. She appeared suddenly beside me as I was bent to the fire, blowing on the smoldering twigs, and asked me if we wanted dry paper. She went back to her camp and kept watching. "Do you want my ax to chop up your logs?" she called across to me. I struggled with the fire until I knew it was useless, then walked over for her ax.

After our fire got going, finally, I asked her to join us, to sit around the fire and make S'mores—chocolate and roasted marshmallow sandwiched between two pieces of graham cracker. She brought over her lawn chair and her tea and settled in. She wouldn't eat a S'more. Too sweet, she said. But she told us stories.

"I used to work as an executive secretary in Manhattan," she said. "Until one day I couldn't stand it anymore. I hated my job. I didn't like myself." She started writing science fiction novels for teenagers and doing other jobs in better places. And then she came to Madeline Island, where she took care of an "elderly gentleman," she said. She loved the island, she said. She loved her job. She loved her life. She loved herself. "I have peace of mind," she said.

I invited her to come down to the beach with us, where we wanted to lie on our backs in the sand and make ourselves dizzy watching the shooting stars and satellites moving across the sky. But she said no. As she picked up her lawn chair and mug of tea and moved away from the light of the fire toward her camp, she said again, "Peace of mind is the most important thing."

There was a mysteriousness, an openness, a sense of generosity about her that made her something more than a casual campfire visitor. I thought later that she had come especially for me, to tell me this thing that I already know, but that I seldom pay attention to.

Craig and I and the girls put all of our berries in a pot and divide them according to our needs—Craig needs more than I do because when the girls visit him he makes blueberry pancakes and muffins. The girls take enough home for their mother to make pies. I take twelve cups of blueberries home. I wash them and put them equally into four bags, three cups to a bag. I am careful with my blueberries, having picked them all so carefully, having suffered mosquito and blackfly bites and scratches and an aching back. I save them for Thanksgiving or Christmas, for the late fall or early winter when the season for blueberries is long past; for when the blueberries are drying into hardened purple jewels, or falling to the ground from their small bushes, feeding grouse and squirrels and mice, or chickadees. I will bake the blueberries into pies and muffins, or make them into syrup or even jam to share with my friends. And I will tell them as they eat where I picked these berries; what kind of day it was, who I was with. And it will make me happy to tell them this, and my happiness will be on their happy purple tongues.

LAKE ONE, LAKE TWO, LAKE THREE, LAKE FOUR

I T WAS THE THIRD WEEK in September and already it had snowed that morning. When I stopped at the U.S. Forest Service ranger station in Ely, Minnesota, the ranger, a woman, said it probably would snow or rain all over the Boundary Waters during the next several days. "Great," I said, rolling my eyes in exasperation. The trip would have been hard enough had the weather been perfect.

For three days before setting out from my apartment in St. Paul I had been in bed with a fever: sweating, coughing and sneezing. A friend told me maybe I should not go on this trip, my first-ever solo canoe trip, in such rotten condition.

"You're sick. Have you ever been sick on a trip? *I* have," she said. "I've heard of people who are sick and feverish going out alone and getting delirious and getting lost."

But I wanted to go. I wanted to go because I had planned all year to go. And I wanted to go to prepare for my future. Upon my return I was to fly to Salt Lake City, Utah, and bury my sister's ashes, finally, almost ten years after her death. This canoe trip was to be a time of openness, a time of meditation, a time of healing. I had prayed, in the awkward and unpracticed way that I pray, to be visited on this trip, by some*one* or some-*thing*, by my sister herself perhaps. I had asked to be taught whatever it was I needed to know in order to be prepared for the task that lay before me.

~

The previous May, on Mother's Day, my mother told me on the telephone that she and my brother Austin had decided it was time to bury Ally's ashes. "Are you crying?" my mother asked me as the phone line buzzed between us.

"Yes," I said. "Yes. Yes. Yes."

She asked me why. Because I was happy, I said. For so long I had wanted us to come together as a family to bury Ally's ashes, and we had not been able to. We had argued over it, and I had cried over it, but we mostly had not talked about it. My mother asked me to start thinking about what we might do to mark this event. We agreed that the coming autumn seemed right, late September, before universities went back to work for the fall. That way we all could be sure and attend.

Immediately, this was my vision: We would all be stylish and somber—better dressed than we had ever been in our lives. I would fly in from Minnesota, my brother Ed and his wife Nancy would fly in from New Mexico. Our father would take a day off from work. Ed and Austin and my father would wear black suits of thin wool. Their black shoes would shine in the sun, planted on the deep green of the late-summer grass. Nancy would wear a blue dress; she would hold Ed's hand. My mother would wear a skirt and a blouse, a string of pearls around her neck. I would wear black silk pants and a gray shirt. Austin's friend Mary would be there (Mary, who did so much of the work when Ally died, making arrangements at the mortuary, slicing the cheese for the gathering we did have), and so would all of my friends and so would all of Ally's far-flung friends, come from California, Seattle and other great distances. There would be a real minister, ministering to us, talking about grief and loss and we would all cry and we would hold each other and tell each other it was all right, that we loved each other, that we missed Ally. We would look grief in the face, looking at grief on each other's faces. We would say, "We still have each other."

At the put-in at Lake One I took my time getting ready, stowing my big Duluth pack in the front of the rented canoe, the little food pack in the back, tucking a clear plastic tarp over it all. Before starting out, I took my own picture by holding the camera away from myself at arm's length. (In the picture my face is close up, almost out of focus, and red and swollen from my sneezing and coughing. The canoe is in the background and you can see snow falling on the water—small pocks for each flake in the smooth lake.)

I set off paddling smoothly, keeping the canoe straight in the water by doing the "J" stroke. When you paddle in the stern on the right-hand side of a canoe, the bow will push to the left. The "J" stroke compensates for that, allowing you to keep your canoe straight in the water without having to switch the side you are paddling on. To do this you curve your paddle outward, away from the canoe, at the end of each stroke. If you get good at it you can do it with a slight twist of your wrist.

After the first ten minutes I was lost, paddling stupidly around a closed, swampy bay, looking for the portage. It takes some remembering, I had to remind myself, it takes some practice to get the hang of what the lakes look like, what a portage looks like and where it might be—a bare, rocky spot hidden in the trees. I got lost twice more. By the time I got to my camp at Lake Two, only three miles from where I had parked my car hours earlier, I was exhausted.

I ground my canoe up onto the graveley beach of the island I had chosen to camp on. It was nearly night and waves had washed foot-thick rust and cream-colored foam up among the big gray rocks at the landing.

I unloaded my Duluth pack, a big sack of a pack, meant to cart unwieldy bulk over short canoe portages. In it I had stuffed everything I might possibly need for my journey—a tent, a sleeping bag, a sleeping pad, a bundle of clothes wrapped in a double layer of brown plastic garbage bags, a tarp, a coil of rope, a set of cooking pots, a cup, a bowl, a plate, silverware, a first-aid kit, a tent repair kit, twine, clothespins, a saw, a small shovel, toilet paper, a tiny stove and fuel.

I unloaded my separate food pack, a small brown day pack filled with more than enough food for my short trip—pasta and rice and coffee and tea and granola bars and candy, a few apples and oranges, tortillas, cheese, cooking oil, foil (in case I caught a fish), spices, sugar, Kool-aid, and a small plastic bottle of half and half.

I dragged the canoe farther up on the gravel and flipped it over, its green petroleum-based bulk practically glowing in the dimming light. I set up my tent, quickly, with wet, cold hands, and then started a fire and sat, chain-smoking Camels in what had now turned to rain. Each time I sucked the hot smoke past my throat into my lungs, it felt like a blanket covering me, making me not care about the weather.

Exhausted, I sat beside the small fire, which I kept alive with wet sticks I managed to heat and partially dry against the pale flames. I would not have been able to start the fire at all had the previous camper at this site not left some birch bark and twigs wrapped in a tattered piece of plastic and neatly tucked beneath a log near the fire grate. Craig's old gray Stetson covered my head, but the hat was soaked through so that my hair was wet. The cuffs of my too-large rain pants were spattered with mud and gummy, wet pine needles; my feet were already soaked from the rivulets that ran over my knees and down into my shoes. I sat, enshrouded in a cloud of cigarette and wood smoke mixed with my own steamy breath rising through the rain-soaked air, and I was afraid—afraid of the dark, afraid of the starless sky, afraid of the tall trees, afraid of the wavy water.

I had not cooked myself any dinner, not wanting to bother with lighting the small Swedish stove, boiling water, and simmering noodles for macaroni and cheese, which was the meal on my menu for this night. All I wanted to do was smoke my cigarettes and stare into the diminishing flames. But my food pack, opened or not, needed to be hung in a tree to keep it away from bears. The only good tree for hanging a pack was tall and old and had a long, strong limb that stretched out over the water.

I moved away from the fire cautiously, childishly afraid something awful might rise up from the black water and take me down with it. I stuck my orange flashlight in my mouth, so I could use both hands to tie my pack onto one end of a long yellow nylon rope, then I searched for a rock to tie to the other end of the rope. Then I stepped back to toss the weighted end of the rope over the tree's strongest limb.

I swung the rock on the end of the rope a few times in order to develop a rhythm, then let the stone and rope loose at precisely the right moment for the stone to soar into the night and then fall back out of the sky, grazing my right cheekbone as I jerked my head away. It drew a drop of blood and made my eyes fill with tears. After several more attempts the stone, yellow rope trailing behind, sailed over the branch and, with a splash, disappeared into the water.

I struggled to concentrate on the details of this task, as if the details, the concentration, would evaporate my fear, the fear that behind me was something terrible, something watching. I had a serious sense of fore-boding, manifested by a tickling on my skin. As my pack was going up into the tree, the nylon rope on the wet bark made animal-like groans each time I pulled, and each time I pulled, the pack jerked crazily. I could see the yellow rope clearly, the knot clearly slipping, the pack clearly fall-ing into the black lake, floating for a moment, then sinking . . .

I imagined it clearly, as if it was one of many ways that moment could have unfolded, given different circumstances, different details, different small actions that added up to a different outcome. What happened re-ally was that I retrieved the stone-weighted end of the rope and pulled, hoisting my pack up into the tree, where it swung in the eerie mist illu-minated by my flashlight. *Everything was fine*, but, I was sure, easily might not have been.

Once in bed I could not sleep. Despite the sheltered, tree-bordered tent space, the wind shook the thin nylon and bent the poles. I heard what I was sure was singing: thin, high, constant, undulating notes that never once stopped. It was not loons, not loons at all. It was not wind in the pines, not wind in the pines at all. It was not even wind curving fast, whistling around rock; not wind and rock at all, but voices, singing, all night long; singing nothing at all, all night long.

During June we had continued to plan for Ally's burial. My mother and father picked out a plot underneath a hawthorn tree in Mt. Olivet Cem-etery in Salt Lake City. "It's a pretty spot," my mother said. "It's the pret-tiest cemetery in Salt Lake." From it you could see out over the valley on a sunny day, clear to the Great Salt Lake. My mother made an appoint-ment with a woman Unitarian minister, despite my father's protests about having an "outsider" involved. When he asked her why we needed a minister, she told him what I had told her: "They are spiritual profes-sionals. That's their job." His reply to her, as she relayed it to me over the telephone, was this: Puzzled, he had said, "But we don't have a spiritual life." After a pause my mother told me, as if it had just then occurred to her to put it exactly this way, "I have a spiritual life! In the spring I watch for the indigo bunting and when I see it my heart leaps up. It really does."

There was confusion over whether my brothers would attend the funeral. Fueled by a fierce determination that we would do this, finally, once and for all, and probably never again, as a *family*, I pressed them, pleaded with them, told them both it was the most important thing in the world to me that they be there. They said to me, all of them, my mother included, in voices that were weird echoes, that, okay, they would come, but they did not plan to cry.

"I've never cried for Ally and I probably never will," said my mother.

"I don't plan to have it be some great emotional purging," said my brother Ed.

I wondered then whether there was something *wrong* with me, something crucial that was genetically askew. I *wanted* to cry. That was the whole point—to cry. And not in private. I *wanted* witnesses to my weeping.

At first, when Ally died, I had grieved quietly, and not understanding what grief was or is, believed it was a thing to be gotten over rather than gone into—a thing to be hidden from, a thing that one kept oneself busy to *avoid*, certainly *not* something one chose to experience on purpose, certainly *not* a beast whose arms you *allowed* to embrace you. In the beginning, I had no models for how to grieve. To *not* cry was the brave thing. To keep oneself *together* was the proper thing. In the letters I wrote to friends then, telling them of Ally's death, I sounded frozen.

Dear Annie, Lisa, Steph and Marylou, I wrote,

My sister Ally died last week. She killed herself with an overdose of anti-depressants. The details seem unimportant to me now. Retelling the story is a waste of time. She is gone. She led a very unhappy life for most of the last six years. We are all trying to tell ourselves that we helped her as much as we could. We tried to understand. None of that seemed to make a difference. . . .

Then in the letter there is something about her sitting on the curb outside the pharmacy before it even opened, putting twenty dollars on the counter, telling the pharmacist, "I want as many of those as this will buy" (What if the pharmacist had said no? What if the pharmacist had been sick that day and hadn't come to open the store?), something about how she lied to Adam, her boyfriend, saying she was going running (What if he had said "I'll go with you"?), about staying home from work (What if they had said, "No, it's a busy day, we need you in the bookstore"?), about a cup beside her bed (What if Adam had come in then, just as she was pouring the pills into her palm, putting the cup to her lips?), something about seizures (What if she had said sooner, "Adam, help me, take me to the hospital"?), something about toxicity in the blood, about blood and the brain, about an angiogram, about a coma, about brain death, about tubes being disconnected.

Despite what I told my friends in the letters, that the details seemed unimportant to me, I did try to tell them the story in all its detail, wishing then that I had more details, angry that I didn't know anything, thinking, my heart thumping, that I should speak to her doctor, get the whole story, get it right—as if knowing what really happened would turn my despair into an answer: This is when she died, this is how she died, this is why she died, this is how you could have saved her.

We are not having a funeral, I wrote proudly in the letters to my friends. *We decided (actually, everyone but me decided because I was not there and I am glad of that) to say goodbye to her in as upbeat a fashion as we know how. And besides that, we've always been a little bit unconventional. We had a gathering at the Art Barn.*

I was fine, I said. Everything was fine. *I howled like an animal for a few days, then I was at peace with myself. I feel relieved. Ally's unhappiness is not a burden for us anymore. I will miss her. It makes me sad. But there is nothing I can do about it now.*

I was holding myself together. At the gathering, those of Ally's friends who wandered around, sobbing and red-eyed, who could not stop crying, who were angry, who clung to my mother or to me, who threw themselves into the deep snow banks outside, they were the strange ones, the ones who had lost control. My father told me that week, the week of the 24th of January, 1985, that he was through grieving, that a friend of his told him he would never get over it, but my father disagreed. He was going back to work. Her body barely gone, the tubes disconnected just days earlier, and already we were getting on with our lives.

In the box containing the letters I wrote then, there are also letters from Ally to me. I find prayers, appeals to spirits, appeals to powers beyond her fast-dwindling own. And I find poems like this one:

> *Smooth Steel Scratch. Stings. Scream Louder.*
> *Can't You Hear Me? Pound. Pounding. Heavier. Slippery*
> *Walls Too High Too Cold.*

And like this one:

> *The gap is open. Fuck! Fill it. No feelings slip.*
> *Slam the lid on. Inject the Drug. Can't escape now.*
> *Fill it. Fill it. Explode! Find another container!*
> *Quick. Fill me.*

The day my father called from Salt Lake City to tell me that my sister was in a coma, I was living in Minnesota with Paul, my boyfriend from Macalester College, in a small apartment above Hoosier's Drugstore on the corner of St. Clair and Snelling. I cried all morning. That evening I was lying in my bed. Paul was in the living room watching the Minnesota Twins on the television. As my vision began to blacken and my breathing began to wane, I could hear the soothing drone of the announcer, the roar of the crowd. I could not breathe. It was as if something was pressing on my chest, preventing me from taking any air into my lungs. I was afraid I was dying. I sprang up and went out to Paul in the living room, and climbed into his lap and he rocked me, in the blue light of the television, late into the night.

The morning of the second day of my canoe trip was again wet and cold and I wanted to go home, but some streak of bullheadedness kept me going—bullheadedness and also the hope that if I stayed in the woods long enough I still might receive some kind of gift, some kind of message about what I was to do when I left the woods and went to Salt Lake City to bury Ally's ashes. I was waiting for some kind of sign.

I went to great lengths that morning to make myself coffee, to which I added a generous amount of half and half (I had kept the cream cold by weighing it down in the water with rocks). I sat on a log facing the lake. Instead of breakfast I lit another cigarette. I smoked and sipped my coffee and looked at my map.

When Craig and I did this trip in the spring of 1986, we had already reached Insula Lake by this time, triple the distance I had come alone. I realized as I looked at the map that I would have to change my plans. I would never make it all the way to Alice Lake. I had wanted to go there to see the pictographs—dim, faded, ocher-colored prints of ancient hands and moose and people in slim canoes, scattered over a great rock wall that rises from the water. There was that voice, rattling on . . . "If you were half the outdoorswoman you claim to be you'd do it. Do it. Do it." Wisely, for once, I chose not to push myself, but instead to move on slowly to Lake Four or just beyond, and then to turn around and return the way I had come.

All day that second day, my canoe was difficult to carry. Normally, you can set the yoke of a canoe on your shoulders and the whole canoe, no matter how heavy, will balance itself. But there was no yoke on my canoe (the man at the outdoors store had told me to put the edge of the seat on my shoulders). For the first four portages of the first day, this was not a problem. But on the second day, with my fatigue, it became almost impossible to balance the canoe. There was more weight in the front of the canoe than in the back, so, with the boat teetering on my shoulders, I had to push up on the bow so that it didn't dip and bang on the rocky trail. Even though my little solo canoe weighed only thirty-five pounds, on my back it felt like an entire house. Eventually, I gave up and began dragging the canoe across the portages, hoping I was not damaging it beyond repair, hoping no one would see me. I realized later that this problem of balance could have been solved had I tied a pair of shoes or a life jacket to the stern in order to weigh it down. But I was not thinking then. I was only moving from Lake One to Lake Two to Lake Three to Lake Four.

In mid-July I called my mother to go over more details regarding the burial of Ally's ashes. I unexpectedly got my father on the phone. After five minutes of pleasantries we got around to the subject of the ceremony and how he really didn't think it was appropriate to invite Ally's friends. They were outsiders. What business was this of theirs? No one, no one but me, he said, really wanted to do this anyway. "The only reason we are doing this is because you insisted," he said. "We're only doing this for you."

"This is something for all of us," I said. I told him he was being mean. "I'm sorry," he said, his voice tight, "but nobody, including you, ever involves me in these things. It's all planned without me." He slammed the phone back into the receiver.

I made camp number two just beyond the rapids that separate Lake Four from Hudson Lake. The day had been swell, when I was not portaging. I learned more and more about how to paddle and steer, how to keep the canoe straight in the water and moving forward at a decent pace, how to conserve energy, how to roll my wrist outward so the paddle made an easy "J" at the end of each stroke. I had stopped frequently during the day to simply sit in my canoe in the middle of the lake and enjoy the water. Every time I stopped I would reach under my rain coat to the breast pocket of my shirt, pull out my cigarettes and light up a smoke. I sat, inhaling, exhaling, flicking the ashes over the gunnel, listening to them hiss as they hit the cold water.

My second night in the woods was uneventful. If I dreamed, I did not know it. If anything visited me, I was unaware of it. The morning came fast, and with it came sun, finally. That morning canoeists skimmed by in the dawn, their boats making hardly a sound, and they smiled at me as I sat drinking my morning coffee by a small fire. The water was too cold for bathing at that time of year, but if it had been warm enough I would have taken off my shirt and my pants and I would have bathed in the amber water just off the smooth rock shelf in front of my camp.

One thing I wanted to make sure of, I told my mother, was that I could take a jar of Ally's ashes back to Minnesota with me. I had a brass urn from India that I wanted to put the ashes in so that I could keep them with me, wherever I might go. Craig and I had bought the urn from a boatman on the Ganges. We had gone down to the steps at Varanasi in the evening and the sun had set around us as we were rowed up the river, and back down, past the fires from the burning bodies in the funeral ghats. And we were sold little lilies with candles in them. "Wishes for the dead and loved ones," the turbanned man who sold them to us had said. We lit the candles in the lilies and the flowers went spinning away in the current. In the morning we went back early to the river and in the rising sunshine we could see people bathing along the river's banks; we could see women washing clothes; and in places we could see the floating bloated carcasses of dead water buffalo. Then up beside us rowed a man selling brass urns. He told me it would hold water from the Ganges, forever, and that Ganges water never went stale. The urn leaked, I found out later, when the pocket of my skirt was soaked through. But it would hold a handful of Ally's ashes.

My mother told me she would get back to me about my request. When we spoke again she told me this: my father had wanted some of Ally's ashes too. But he decided against it. And this is why, my mother said: the bodies are often not wholly burned when they are cremated. Sometimes in the ashes there are bits of bone, maybe part of a tooth. "Identifiable fragments," she called them, no doubt repeating my father's phrase, my father's fear. She relayed this like a warning. I told her I didn't care. I knew Ally was dead. And I knew the ashes for what they were—a portion of the leftover mass of her once beautiful body.

On the third day of my canoe trip I ran out of cigarettes at about noon. I had planned to paddle back to Lake One and camp there, within easy distance of the put-in point, to spend one last night in the woods. But with no cigarettes, the rest of the trip seemed pointless. I wouldn't be able to sit on a log by the fire and smoke. I'd have to endure the itchy-throated, jumbly, nervous feeling of not having a smoke when I wanted one. I'd have to just sit still and do nothing.

I concocted a ridiculous plan. I paddled all the way back to Lake One. I unpacked my canoe and set up my tent, then got back into my canoe and paddled to the put-in, got out of my canoe, got into my car, drove to the nearest resort, purchased the very last, stale, end-of-the-season pack of Marlboro Reds for sale behind the glass panes of the oaken case, drove back to Lake One, got back into my canoe and paddled to my camp. This took me two hours; two hours I could have used to quietly contemplate the woods. Two hours I could have used to sit still, to empty myself and prepare to be filled.

By the time I got back to my camp, a wind had come up, flapping the sleeves of my jacket, shaking the tent. I suspected a storm, so I ran about, weighing down the tarp I had thrown over my gear, covering the firewood. I tried to light the stove. I splashed gas on the ground and on the stove. When I lit it, the whole thing burst into flames.

That night, there I was again, hunched up over the fire grate, smoking, drinking tomato soup from a mug, thinking how silly it had been to bring all that food. I sighed, remembering that I had to hang the food pack before I could go to sleep. I looked around for a tree to hang it from, but quickly turned my gaze back to the fire, to the warm coals, to the close-up space of the fire grate, to my small stove, to my boots drying in front of the flames, to the logs that surrounded the fire. To look beyond the confines of that space made me feel lost.

Somewhere near the end of August I spoke to my mother yet again. "I don't like to hurt people," she said right off. There would be no ceremony, she said. She didn't want to do it. My brothers didn't want to do it. No one but me wanted to do it. "We have never been conventional," she said. As if this was a matter of consistency. *This was no time to change our ways.* "We just don't *do* this kind of thing," she said. As if having a funeral was bad manners somehow, like dancing on tables drunk.

I screamed at her, croaking, crying, frothing at the mouth, calling her a coward—my own mother I called a coward! "Why can't we do this?" I pleaded over and over. "Just this once can't we do this, together, please?" Even as I pleaded I realized the futility of my begging, but I also knew in that instant that I would go ahead and bury her ashes by myself if I had to. I would do it alone.

"It would just be too hard for your father," my mother said.

My last morning in the woods, I dawdled. I sat on a granite boulder that jutted out into the lake, with my coffee and my pack of cigarettes. I smoked and drank coffee and watched canoeists coming by on their way back to their cars. They waved. I waved back. "Beautiful day!" they said. Yes. The sun was coming out. We joked across the water about the sun. It had been a rainy and cold few days.

I tried to take stock. I tried to focus on what I might have learned from this solo canoe trip. I realized one true thing about myself on this trip. I enjoy solitude, but I do not enjoy being alone. I need the company of others. I yearn for contact. I want to be touched, I want to be kissed, I want to be held close, to have my hair caressed, my cheekbones softened by loving fingertips, to feel around myself at night the warm arms of a lover. But not *just* a lover. Family too. Friends. Connections. Connections that work like soft knots holding me down to my place in the world.

Other people are the most important thing. *Relations*, connections, contact with other live creatures—that is the most important thing. I sat on the rock at the edge of the lake thinking of Ally's death. If you could not grieve this, the most horrible thing that could ever happen to you in your life—having someone you love die, disappear, turn to ash, never, ever to return in the flesh—then what *was* important? If this did not interrupt your life, if this failed to make you cry, if not this, what?

Back at Lake One, at the end of my trip, there were men at the landing, grizzled and stubble-faced from weeks in the woods, and I asked them to help me get my canoe up the shore and onto my car, and they said sure and hoisted it up just so, their celebratory cigars burning between their lips. It was snowing again. In my car, I cranked up the heater so that each snowflake that landed on the windshield evaporated instantly.

On the way back to Ely I saw a wolf. It didn't scare me, but I was shocked to see it out like that in the open: right out there along the road, where everyone could see it, in plain daylight. It had crossed the road in front of me, gray-yellow and lanky, and hid from me for a moment in the grass beside the road. I stopped, pulling off onto the shoulder across from it and it stared at me for a while, its ears perked up high. Then it climbed out of the ditch and trotted down the road behind me, zig-zagging across the asphalt, stopping once to look back and see my car. After it disappeared around a corner, I pulled out into the road and drove on.

At the ranger station, where I stopped one last time before heading back to the city, I told the ranger about the wolf. She said this was common, especially on that piece of road. "Oh yes, people see wolves out there all the time," she said. "They are all over the place." It was nothing to fear.

The next few days I spent unpacking my canoe gear and preparing for the ceremony. I made calls, frantically trying to track down Ally's old friends. They would want to know, I reasoned. They would want to be there. They would drop whatever they were doing, I knew it, and they would come flying in for the day.

I was like a detective, calling the last number I had in my address book, calling directory assistance in Salt Lake City, Seattle, San Francisco, writing down ten numbers with the correct last name, trying them all. "Yes, sorry, I have the wrong number, thank you," I said over and over. After many castings into the wide electronic net, I managed to get numbers for Renee, Adam and Mona. Adam was not home. I sent him a note instead, via overnight mail. Mona was married and lived in California. I left a message on her answering machine. Renee I reached at a remote Forest Service outpost on the Green River in Utah.

"Renee?" the person on the other end replied. "Wait a minute." I heard a screen door creak open and slam shut. I heard crickets chirp, the rush of water, the heavy steps of boots on hard ground.

"Renee," I said, "this is Gretchen . . . Legler."

He told me he was married, now. He told me that Ally's death messed him up for a long time. Now he was better. He didn't think he could make it to a ceremony. He was sorry. It would be impossible, really. He reminded me that it had been a long time. He wasn't sure it was such a good idea to come anyway. He was better now.

I counted the participants on my fingers. One, two, three; three of my friends from high school said they would definitely come. Of course, they had said, without a second thought. My mother had said she'd probably not be there but still might change her mind; four. My brother Austin, who lived in town, said he had to work, but could probably get a few hours off; five. My brother Ed would not be flying in. I had not heard from my father. I would make six, if everything went as planned.

Although I felt I had no idea how to proceed, I began to collect objects and to plan. From the tanned hide of the deer I had shot a year before I made a small leather pouch. I cut two ovals from the soft leather and stitched them together with red thread, pushing the needle through each thickness with the help of a thimble. From more hide I cut an "A" for Ally and sewed it on the outside of the pouch with red thread. Then I brushed the leather with cedar oil, which stained it a deep brown and made it smell like canoe country in autumn.

I set up an altar on my desk, on top of and around my computer, with candles and pictures of Ally—one of her strong and tan and long-legged with mountains rising behind her and her hands in the pockets of her khaki shorts; one of her smiling, the fall before she died, sitting in my rocking chair in the apartment above the drugstore on Snelling Avenue. I played music, and as I filled the pouch with items scattered around me I told her what each one was for and where it came from:

A pair of gold and black African earrings, which I had bought two pairs of so that we could wear identical sets.

The iridescent purple and green feathers from the tail of a drake mallard I had shot and cooked and eaten.

A piece of iron ore from deep inside a mine in northern Minnesota.

A picture of me and Cate.

A picture of Craig and me at our wedding.

"You would have liked them all," I said aloud.

Then I put in a sprig of sage and a sprig of lavender from my garden, and a tiny bell. "For you to ring, if you ever come around," I said.

I had arranged to stay with my high-school friend Steph and her husband Eric and their son, on the other side of the city from my parents' house in Salt Lake City. "This will hurt your father," my mother said. "He won't understand."

The day before the ceremony, my mother and I drove from our respective houses and met at the cemetery where she showed me the grave, under the hawthorn tree. She showed me the office, where I was to go the next morning at ten o'clock to pick up the basket, which was to have in it the plastic box of ashes, which were to be covered by a lace doily. Everything was all set, my mother said. She had taken care of the details. There would be flowers, a bouquet of white lilies and roses, delivered to the site.

We went back to my parents' house, where I had told my father I would be most of the day, sitting on the porch, in case he wanted to see me. While we sat, my mother and I, I told her my plans for the ceremony. I felt as if I might as well have been reading her a grocery list, so emotionless was my voice. I asked her if she wanted to add anything to the leather bag that I would put into Ally's grave. She brought me a seashell from Australia that Ally had kept with others in a shoebox in the closet of the bedroom we had shared as girls. My mother handed me the shell hesitantly, as if she might draw it back, or as if she was then thinking of other things to include instead. She seemed as unsure as I about what to do.

As the evening before the ceremony progressed, I started to panic. There should be a candle. I drove quickly to a shopping mall and picked a small square glass votive and a candle to go inside. There should be music. I asked to borrow Steph's boombox. The batteries were dead. Eric hurried out to the store for more. Still the box didn't work. He took it apart and fixed it, with me all the while saying, "Don't worry about it. I don't need it." But he insisted. I wondered what else I could be missing.

That night, as I lay in bed on Steph's back porch in Salt Lake City, not far from the house where Ally had lain, swallowing the pills that killed her; not far from the hospital where she died, I expected, again, to be visited by her—at least to dream about her on the eve of her burial. But nothing came.

When Steph and Marylou and I arrived at the cemetery, Rob was there, shaking hands with my father and brother Austin under the hawthorn tree. And there was my mother in a navy blue suit, and Ed with his arm around her, and Nancy by Ed's side. And Renee had come, and Mona, and Adam had gotten the overnight mail note and he had come too. They had all come early and were waiting for us, watching me as I walked slowly to the graveside, the basket that held the ashes in my hand. . . .

My father *could* have decided to walk over from his lab, just on the other side of the football stadium parking lot. He *could* have decided to come. And Austin *might* have asked his boss for the day off. My mother, too, *might* have changed her mind at the last moment and decided not to stay home and make orange marmalade. For an instant I saw them all there, all of us in a half-circle under the tree, our hands at our faces, dabbing our eyes with tissue, looking down at the granite stone that lay beside the hole in the earth: Allison K."Ally" Legler. August 28, 1962 – January 15, 1985.

What *really* happened was that there was a man talking to Rob, un-folding chairs and placing them on the kelly green fake carpet, asking Rob how many to set out, and Rob was holding up four fingers.

Rob and Steph and Marylou watched me nervously, waiting for cues. I put the tape in the boombox, but forgot to turn it on. Steph asked me, "Should we turn on the music?" I said yes. We sat in the folding chairs. I took the candle out of my bag and lit it. I began to read from a scrap of paper I had been carrying around, thinking that I might read what was on it at Ally's ceremony, but only that instant deciding it was the right thing to do. I read:

In the British Museum of London there is something called the papyrus of Ani, which came from Egypt in late 18th century B.C. It is a story in pic-tures of Anubis, the wolf or jackal-headed Egyptian deity who assisted Osiris with the final judgement of souls. It was the duty of Anubis to weigh the heart of every person on the scales of justice. If the heart balanced a feather, a symbol of truth, the person was saved.

This was my way of saying that I knew my sister had been saved; saved by virtue of her goodness, saved by virtue of her truthfulness. She was not the kind of person who would end up in Hell.

Rob read a poem he had written about Ally called "Winterkill:"

> *One month ago you said you wouldn't,*
> *a week ago you registered at the U.*
> *now I read your name in the Sunday Tribune,*
> > *. . . died Jan. 15, after a long battle*
> > *with the realities of life.*
>
> *Are you so impulsive that you reached*
> *for the bottle just to spite the doctors*
> *you hated. Were you lying to me*
> *like you lied to them, or did you know.*

Last week when you seemed so at peace,
you knew,
> *having made up your mind.*
> *I misread your calm resolve.*
I'm proud of you, I said, and you winked.

Next Marylou asked if I would mind if she said a prayer. I said that of course she should pray. "Heavenly Father. . . ." she began, and as she asked for good things for my sister, and for relief for me and my family, her voice grew deeper, softer, her breathing changed. She lay a bouquet of chrysanthemums on Ally's grave.

Steph too spoke and cried. And then I bent to one knee and drew the green carpet back and revealed the neat square hole of dirt and took the box of ashes in both hands and placed it there in the earth. I uncorked a bottle of water from the Ganges and sprinkled it around. I took pinches of tobacco and sprinkled them on the box of ashes. Rob hesitated, then reached for the tobacco pouch and did the same. Steph and Marylou followed suit. We were all embarrassed, I think, not knowing what to do first, then second, then third. I took dirt from the pile next to the square hole and sprinkled it, listening as the fine dirt landed softly on the box of ashes. My friends took handfuls of dirt and repeated the action. I left the hole uncovered. I did not draw the green carpet back over it. I did not want to try and cover anything up.

I asked Steph then, as we hugged each other, if it would be improper to take pictures. She said I could do anything I wanted, so we traded the camera back and forth and took pictures of each other in groups, holding each other, red-eyed and smiling sadly.

When I arrived at my parents' house after the ceremony, Austin was on the back porch, sipping a beer, talking with my mother. He was relaxed, sitting in a lawn chair, stretched out in his urban cowboy way, his pointed boots crossed over one another, his rugged face partly in the sun. Inside, on top of the kitchen counter, stood the lined-up small jars of marmalade my mother had made that morning. The marmalade hadn't turned out exactly right, she told me. It didn't quite set.

I gave my mother the one white rose she had asked for from the bouquet that had lain on Ally's tombstone, and I gave her the woven basket she had requested, the one in which I carried the box of ashes to the graveside. After I had given her these, my brother said: "I'm glad we did this."

"Where *were* you?" I asked him.

"I forgot the time," he said. "I looked up and it was late." He had tried to meet us at the cemetery, he said, but we had already left.

"It was supposed to be at ten o'clock," I said.

"Oh," he said. "I got there at eleven."

Where *were* you? I wanted to ask him again and again and again.

"Someone left a book of poetry," he said.

"Yes," I said. "That was Rob."

"And a bouquet of mums," he said.

"That was Marylou," I said.

"And there was a lit candle there in a tiny glass container," he said.

"Yes," I said. "That was me."

Months later Austin called me to talk about love and family. He had joined a group that was making him see the world differently, he said. I could tell. The phone call was proof enough of that. "Don't give up on our family," he said. "There's still hope."

I asked him, "Where have you been?" I held the telephone away from my face and yelled into it as if into a megaphone. "Where were you when I needed you to help bury our sister?"

"Asleep," he said.

"I don't want to hear what you have to say about family," I said.

"I've been asleep," he said, "for a long time."

Around the same time as Austin's call, I received a letter from my mother in which she explained to me, kindly, why she and my father did not join me in burying Ally's ashes. She was aware, she said, of my great disappointment. She wrote:

As the years go by you learn to close doors on unpleasant memories. You know they're there but you don't go digging around in that old closet, digging out the ugly, the bruised and battered experiences of your life. You have to learn to refocus on what's good in life. I've tried to concentrate on my gardening, which I enjoy very much, and on feeding and identifying birds. I've also made it a point to be nice to the people whose services I enjoy on a daily basis—the janitor, the mailman. I try to make other people's days a little brighter.

So the problem with the ceremony was that we had completed our mourning for Ally, gone through a long and painful healing process and come to an acceptance of our loss that we could live with. It became tortuous for us to imagine going through it again. I remember your saying to me, "But you saw her die." I'm supposing that you meant that that brought a reality to us that you couldn't share. That's something you will have to work out for yourself, Gretty. I don't have any answers to that one. Sometimes we are faced with the difficult task of risking hurting some people we love dearly to protect another we love just as dearly. In this case we hurt you to protect ourselves. I hope that you will understand.

Later still, I received word from my friend Marylou that she had questions about the ritual we four friends had performed beside Ally's grave. It had seemed occultic to her, and in her mind was linked with my being a lesbian. She asked why I put tobacco on Ally's grave. Did it have anything to do with me starting smoking again? Was it true that most lesbians smoked and were alcoholic? Why had I shaved my head, was this a rite of passage, did it have something to do with goddess worship? Why did I say what I said about Egyptian deities and having a light heart, she wanted to know. Was it possible to have a light heart and also to truly love? To truly love, she said, is to face and endure sorrow and grief along with joy. It was not possible, was it, to have a light heart?

And then finally, months after the ceremony, I got word from my sister.

The visit from her that I had gone canoeing alone for, the instructions I had wanted so badly before I buried her ashes, came quietly, in a dream. In the dream, I was in Germany watching a parade. In the very front of the parade, leading the jugglers and the acrobats and the colorful floats, was a taller-than-life amazon of a woman, tanned and blue-eyed and blonde-haired. Her hair was short and as bright as the sun and she was flipping and dancing and twirling a baton. As she passed me I realized it was my sister. After the parade I followed her to a small house, like a fairy-tale cabin, tucked behind a picket fence in a quiet neighborhood. There were green shutters on the windows. When I walked up the sidewalk she was watering red geraniums in her window box.

"Come home with me," I said.

"I like it here," she said. "I had to get out of there. I'm not going back."

She didn't say it fiercely or bitterly, but with resolve. She smiled as she said it. She said it as if she were sorry for me.

THIS RIVER AT NIGHT

T HIS RIVER AT NIGHT is full of moving light.

We are sitting on the bank of the McKenzie River in Oregon. During the day, when I walked here, a man stood in the middle of the current, up to his thighs in water, a creel at his hip, casting a fly. Now, at midnight, there is no one else around. Just you and me.

Across the water a man and a woman and their friends have gone to bed, and turned off the porch light on their cabin. "Goodnight, goodnight," they called to one another, and then there was, for a second, utter darkness, until my eyes adjusted.

In the cedar woods on the bank I can hardly see your face in the dark. I am a little afraid. I look over my shoulder now and then, afraid we are being watched. I sense a presence in the woods. But you tell me to relax. You are telling me about being afraid of water, about a trip you took, about snorkeling, about a barracuda in the sea. "They hang in the ocean," you say. "Their eyes are this big." I have to reach out and feel the circle you have made with your fingers, to see this big barracuda eye.

This river with no lights is the color of jade, and white shades move over it like ghosts. In the day, when I came here, I could see that these places of dancing whiteness are places where water froths around logs, over rocks. But at night with no lights, when you can't see the tree branches or the boulders, the white spaces move as if nothing at all is encouraging their curving, their shifting, their

177

disappearing and reappearing.

On the bank, in a mess of fern and clover, you start to shiver. A cold damp is rising up from the water. Now you are telling me about riding your bike in Forest Park in Portland, which is where you live, and about how getting caught in the park in the dark doesn't scare you. Really.

This is all about light, I think. How it scares and soothes us; fascinates us; hides and reveals. All around us the cedars, their branches covered with hairy hanging moss, glow green-gray in the darkness.

Later, well past midnight, we walk to my room, you leading the way out of the woods, along the uneven path, slowly, reaching behind your back for my hand. You tell me you don't want to turn on your flashlight because it would spoil the night. We leave the curtains open and the windows ajar. In the dark, the white sheets glow. The thin arcs of hair over your eyes are black; your eyes are black; your brown hair is black; the hollows under your arms and this place between your thighs are black. And when you turn, white shadows roll across your belly.

ALL THE POWERFUL

INVISIBLE THINGS

All God's critters got a place in the choir
Some sing low
And some sing higher
Some sing out loud on a telephone wire
And some just clap their hands ...

CAROLYN AND I ARE SINGING. It is sunny out and we are raking
oak and birch and maple leaves into mountainous piles. It is May
and the snow has just melted and the leaves are all brown and wet. We
are part of the work crew at Camp Van Vac. In exchange for food and
lodging for the weekend, Carolyn and I and our friends, along with a
handful of others, are helping the owners do all of the work that needs to
be done before the resort opens in a week or two for guests. This weekend
we will rake paths, re-roof cabins, lift the canoes down out of the rafters
of the boathouse, sweep the spider webs from the corners of the outhouses, split kindling for the wood stoves and restock the wood boxes on
the cabin hearths.

Carolyn's and my instructions are to clean the resort's winding dirt
paths of leaves and to rake around the base of each cabin so that the ac-
cumulation of wet leaves doesn't rot the logs. Our other friends, Cheryl
and Ellen and Wendy, are off doing other chores. This is good labor. It is

good to be out in the sun and to be singing. As I work, belting out verses to *The Sound of Music* and *Camelot*, I glance up now and then to watch Carolyn. I harbor a ridiculous hope, despite what happened the night before, that if I sing loud and well enough I will get Carolyn to love me.

"*Yeeoow!*" Carolyn screams. I drop my rake and run to her, afraid she has stepped on glass or cut her eye on a twig. But she has raked up a tiny frog. She bends down to pick it up and I touch it in the palm of her hand. It is as still as an ice cube. She puts the frog in the sun by a warm metal barrel and in about a minute it is jumping back into its safe, cool cave of leaves. It amazes me that the frog should be there, invisible and as cold as winter under the leaves.

I ask Carolyn what kind of frog it is. She says she doesn't know. I expect her to know all the names of the animals in the woods, and the names of plants too, and of stars. She is getting a degree in conservation biology. I think of her as an expert.

If she had said anything else at all the night before, I would have dropped it, this wanting her. I would have realized that singing wouldn't help at all, that nothing would make her my lover. But the night before, she took my hand and held it in hers and said, "I am so lucky." As we rake and sing I am still clinging to those words, having not listened at all to the rest of what she said. I make those four specific words mean exactly what I want them to mean—that she will come to me some day. Those four words hold my hope, like cupped hands holding water.

The previous night the five of us had driven up from Minneapolis, completing the six-hour drive at around midnight. Along the way I dozed in the back of the van, with my head in Ellen's lap, feeling her gently touch my hair, listening to her and Wendy quietly reminisce about their travels in the southwest. Carolyn's and Cheryl's soft women's voices traveled back to me from the front seat, reminding me of when I was a child and the sound of my parents' voices in conversation filled our car in exactly the same way, anchoring me.

We all pressed our faces to the windows of the van when Carolyn said that there were northern lights. The sky was full of them; full of dancing lights, full of pale green sheets. I imagined them then as the flowing skirts of goddesses, moving among the stars like fabric in the wind.

The northern lights were still out, still moving, when we pulled down the narrow drive into Camp Van Vac. After putting our bags away in the big cabin the five of us were to share, Carolyn and I walked out onto the point. The point is a jumble of greenstone jutting out into the lake, where you can sit and catch the wind, or listen to the ice go out, or feel night sounds—a late-calling loon and water against rock.

Across the lake, the green and yellow and cream colored lights of the aurora still danced. As I watched, in my imagination I too danced and twisted and loomed among the veils. I too was some spirit dancing around a fire, my body lit from the inside by flame.

We were sitting on the rock, close enough so that our knees and shoulders touched. Carolyn pointed out stars to me—the Northern Cross, the sickle and the Archer. I pointed out the ones I knew: the North Star, the Big and Little Dipper. I sipped from a styrofoam cup of port and munched on a ginger snap.

Port and ginger snaps and sitting out on the point at Camp Van Vac at night were part of a ritual I had worked up. It was a relatively new ritual, only in its second year. Not a tradition yet, but something that seemed important that I repeat, on this night especially. I told Carolyn how happy I was to be here, how I used to come here with Craig when we were married and how it had been two years now since I had left him and how I had come back both of those years—first with Cate and now with her and the others, my friends—and I couldn't be happier *and, and, and* . . .

Soon enough, because Carolyn was so quiet and because when I looked at her she was staring at her feet, I realized that my voice had become annoying. My urgent need to mark this time, to make this time something monumental for me, was too much for her.

"Sometimes it's good to just be," she said. "Sometimes being so self-conscious takes us away from where we are." All of a sudden I was ashamed. I would have blushed if it had not been so cold out.

For a while we sat without talking, then she began, in the low, smooth voice that I have always thought matched the darkness of her hair and eyes, the broadness of her shoulders, to tell me a story that came from the time she worked with Wilderness Inquiry and was out with a handful of kids on a canoe trip.

One of the boys on the trip had mild mental retardation. Another of the boys had autism. As is common with people who have autism, this boy organized his life by a series of rituals: to bed every night at the same time; breakfast every morning just so. The boy's routine was sometimes maddening; he needed absolute regularity, Carolyn said, and he was always checking his watch to see that he was doing the right thing at the right time. He had received tremendous love and care, she said, and could report in writing whether he was happy or mad or sad, but, as is also common in people with autism, could go no further in explaining or examining his feelings.

One night the northern lights came up brilliantly, Carolyn said. She and the kids lay back on their sleeping bags on their flat rock point, a point like the one she and I sat on as she told me this story, and gazed unbelievingly at the sky. All except the boy with autism, who, as the lights were coming on, folded his clothes, combed his hair, brushed his teeth and climbed into his bag.

After they had watched the lights for some time, the boy who had mild mental retardation asked Carolyn if she could write something for him. He wanted to tell his mother about the lights, he said. He wanted to tell her how powerful, marvelous and unbelievable the lights were. Carolyn took out a pad of paper and a pencil and took it all down:

Dear Mother, we are on West Bearskin Lake watching northern lights. They are green and red and blue and yellow. The lights are all over the sky, moving. I wish you could see them. I love you.

After a while, Carolyn said, she and the boy and the rest of them became bored, confused. What do you do after you have looked at such an awesome thing for so long? You must, at some point, stop and get into your sleeping bag and close your eyes. What else is there? There isn't any way, is there, to go to the lights? You always must go back to your own particular life with a vague ache in your heart; an ache that suggests to you there is another place you should be, although you don't know where it is.

As Carolyn finished her story, she tilted her head back to look up at the sky and I saw a silver strand of tear snake its way over her sharp cheekbone and down the side of her neck, into the hollow of her shoulder. Suddenly, I thought that I had to tell Carolyn that I loved her. I had to seize that moment and tell her something. Anything.

Our knees and hands had become stiff from the cold. We rose, helping each other up, and we made our way back toward our cabin along a dirt trail crisscrossed with the shadows of thin birch. We rounded a corner and from a distance through the trees I saw the light from the window of the cabin, yellow and safe. Our friends were there sitting around the wood stove, talking. Before we got to that light, before the light broke the bond that the night had created between us, I had to tell her.

I turned around suddenly so that Carolyn stopped short of running right into me. I touched her face and said, stuttering and halting, "I've been attracted to you." I felt ridiculous, light-headed, kicking myself already for the banality of what had just come out of my mouth. "And I've been struggling with what to do about it," I said. "And I decided a long time ago that the most important thing to me was to be your friend." This *had* been true, but at that moment was not true at all. I wanted her as my lover. I was lying even as I was trying to tell the truth.

Carolyn took my hand and said to me, "I am *so* lucky," and we hugged each other. Then I held her as she turned toward the lake, so that my body pressed into her back, and I could feel the heat of her through her jacket and wool shirt and she started to cry and we stood like that looking out at the water. Soon we were both shivering, and we walked back to the cabin.

Ellen was still up and we sat with her in the hot orange light that made the cabin walls glow gold. Carolyn talked, nervously, I thought, about her work, about seed patents and genetically engineered plants. I was afraid that I had scared her and that what she was doing was trying to put words between us: hard-edged words and ideas.

Finally, she lay down to sleep on the floor beside the cot I was lying on, in front of the fire, and I asked her if I could lie next to her for a while. She said yes. I asked her if I could touch her. She said yes. I ran my hands through her thick hair, again and again. Her face showed up against the firelight, ruddy, sharp and full. I touched her cheeks, ran my fingers across from bone to bone, pausing, fingers trembling, at her lips. I touched her collarbone, my fingers like feathers, brushing the length of it.

I asked her if she had ever kissed a woman. No, she said. I asked her if she had ever loved me. How? she said. As a lover, I said. No, she said. I told her I had known her for long enough to know that she was one woman I could be with forever. She asked me, in a sleepy voice, what exactly these qualities were that I thought she possessed and I told her to never mind what I said, it was all right, and I ran my hand through her hair again. I asked her how this felt. How what feels? she said. When I touch you, I said. It feels friendly, she said. I told her it didn't feel that way to me and I stopped. It was wrong to touch her like that if we weren't both in it together. I told her I loved her and she smiled and then I said goodnight and went back to my cot.

> *Swing low, sweet chariot*
> *Coming for to carry me home*
> *Swing low, sweet chariot*
> *Coming for to carry me home.*
>
> *I looked over Jordan and what did I see*
> *Coming for to carry me home?*
> *A band of angels coming after me*
> *Coming for to carry me home.*

Carolyn sings these verses out loud and deep in her clear voice. I join in later, softly, almost under my breath. I apologize all morning, until I know I don't need to do it anymore, until I know that she forgives me and that it is all right. We rake and sing songs from Broadway musicals—from *Fiddler on the Roof*, from *The Music Man*, every musical tune and every bad campfire song we can remember. We sing spirituals, even Christmas carols, any song we can think of that sounds happy, and we see the frog and we make big piles of leaves and sit in the leaves together and talk and I know that everything will be fine between us.

Even as I am still in love with her, as I hang on to the hope of having her as a lover, I feel as if I have been saved by her. Anything could have happened the night before. Instead, I was saved by her. It was as if I had jumped out of a canoe on a windy day, on purpose, just to see what she'd do, and she didn't pull me back in, but instead threw me a life jacket. She didn't foolishly come in after me, to get wet and cold too, and maybe even drown with me, but she threw me the life jacket and told me, "Put it on."

All morning long as we rake and sing, I feel as if Carolyn has pointed out to me the shape of an idea—the ghostliest outlines of a concept—the idea of the difference between a friend and a lover. I squint hard when I think about it, staring into the bushes, or at the mortar between the stones of the foundation of the cabin I am raking around. I stand there, on the shady side of the cabin, raking at a clump of leaves still embedded in ice, smelling the rich mildew coming up from the leafy earth, squinting, trying to focus on the idea, so that next time I will recognize it all on my own. All day I feel like I am walking around something, something that has mass and weight, something that has shape, that has color, but that I can't see yet. When I do see it I don't even know what it will be.

The five of us take the afternoon off from raking and chopping and stacking and hauling to go into Ely to visit the International Wolf Center. At the center, I follow the curving walls of an elaborately laid-out display, pushing buttons to hear wolves howl, flipping through plastic-sheathed pages of thick books about werewolves and wolf-men and wolves who ate children and wolves who lovingly raised children. I read about St. Francis and the wolf, about wolves in sheep's clothing, about the Lamb of God. I look at pictures of wolves fornicating with maidens, wolves with their dreadful, lustful tongues hanging out.

I am particularly taken with a display of pictures and stories elaborating pre-Christian myths about wolves. I stand, my work-blistered hands clasped behind my back, my dusty, booted feet apart, reading from an illustrated panel on the wall all about the Scandinavian story of Fenris.

Fenris, the wolf, offspring of the gods, must be bound by a magical cord to restrain his destructive impulses. The cord that binds him seems as light as gossamer, but in truth it is unbreakable. The cord is made from the powerful invisible things of the world, such as the breath of fish, the roots of mountains, the noises of cats when they move, the beards of women, the anguish of bears, the yearning of glaciers, the voices of red leaves as they fall. When the world is about to end, according to the myth, Fenris will break loose and devour the world and the gods. And then a new and better world will b...

I marv... ...ent stories that I go on to read, mak-
i... ...lay. These are stories so powerful
t... ...time they made perfect sense of an
er... ...how a simple thing, a wolf, is made
co... ...d me of how an ordinary thing is
ma... ...so much larger than itself. And
the ... ...e word. The stories we tell about
each ... ...own lives, about wolves and the world around us,
join together to form some kind of invisible narrative net that is thrown
over us, binding us all.

At dinner back at the resort, all of us at the work weekend share stories
of our accomplishments: a new roof is up on cabin eleven, the wood crew
split two cords of birch, the sauna and shower floor has a new layer of
blue paint, the paths up to cabin twenty are leaf-free.

After dinner, Carolyn and I walk around the point and look at birds.
She has the bird book and is looking up into the birches and pines, which
I see now, looking through binoculars, are full of birds, so many small
yellow and brown birds, as dense as Christmas lights. I want to know
what they are. Carolyn tells me she thinks there are at least two different
kinds of warblers—a male Cape May Warbler and Palm Warblers, whose
sex she can't determine.

Finally, we sit down on the rocks of the point in the windy evening
sunshine. Around us the warm rock gives off a dusty, flinty smell. A
bird zings past me at eye level, fifty yards out into the lake, and I ask
Carolyn, pointing, my outstretched arm and finger following the bird
around to my right, "What is that?" She doesn't know. "Is it in your book?"
I ask. "I don't know," she says, then she is quiet for a while and I hear the
wind in the tall pines behind us. There is that smell again, dusty and
sweet; the smell of the drying surface of the earth and thin, warm yel-
low-white sun.

She is sitting back holding up her strong torso with her arms propped
behind her. Her bluejean-covered legs are crossed. Her brow is creased
just a little bit, and her mouth is set in a straight line. I ask her what she

is thinking. She says this: "Sometimes I think we observe and name not to find out what is there where we are, but to try to figure out whether we are in the right place." She is talking about herself as much as me. It is the most frenzied observers of the surface who miss the most in the depths. I know what she means. It is those who are most meticulous at recording observable phenomena who miss the faces of the dead when they visit, the importance of dreams, the sweetness of water. It is those who name the most and the hardest who are least aware of where they are.

Early the next morning, before the others are awake, I walk outside and pee, squatting in the bushes beside the cabin. I look out at the lake and it is gray and frothing. I walk around to the front of the cabin and wake Carolyn, who is bundled in her sleeping bag on the ground. She wanted to sleep outside, she said, to be out there when the sun came up.

She and I hurriedly dress and paddle out into the lake in a canoe. We are headed toward an island where I had hidden two small deer-hide-wrapped packages the previous spring. I had asked Carolyn earlier, on our way up to Camp Van Vac, if she would go to the island with me. There was something special I had to do there, I told her, and I needed her help. Even on a still day I wouldn't want to paddle it alone, and today with the wind and waves there would be no way I could make it out and back by myself.

The spring I put the packages on the island, shielding them with a piece of birch bark, nestling them in the deep moss under some blue-berry bushes, I had tried to motor out to the island. I had a new metal Grumman canoe with a square stern and a 2.5-horsepower motor. The motor stopped half way across the lake and I couldn't get it started again. Every time I primed it, gas pooled out into the lake and Cate, who was with me, got angry and then sad and told me to just stop trying because I was getting gas in the lake.

So the two of us paddled and Cate waited in the canoe for me while I got out on the island and lit a candle and put the bundles under the blue-berry bushes and said a prayer. The prayer was a hope that, sometime, what was hurting me so much then would hurt less, and that in the meantime this place was safe and sacred and a good place to lay these parcels.

Back at the dock at Camp Van Vac, Cate and I were unloading the canoe when I fell in. I was lifting the tiny motor off of the back of the canoe, and the canoe tipped and I went sideways, my whole body, parka, hat, boots and motor, into the five-foot-deep icy water. I came up sputtering, gasping and afraid, water dribbling off my hat brim. Cate told me to run, run to the cabin and get out of my wet clothes. I was standing naked in front of the wood stove when Cate came in finally, laughing, to rub me warm with a soft towel.

The deer-hide-wrapped bundles were all about a woman named Anna, who showed me what it was like, for the first time in my life, to love myself. In them I put small sacred things—a love poem, a picture, chocolate, a vial of water from the Ganges, silk scarves, silk panties, a small red piece of iron ore, a sprig of sage—ordinary things dense with meaning only for me.

It is hard paddling and Carolyn is having a difficult time keeping the canoe straight in the wind. Waves are breaking over the bow. My shoes are already wet and my arms ache. The idea in going out to the island this time is that everything is over between Anna and me, and I will bury the bundles deep because this door on her has been shut.

At first when I put them there and I told Anna about it, she cried and said she didn't want to be buried, and I said no, no, I didn't bury you, that wasn't it, I had only put them under a piece of bark, for safekeeping, until I knew what to do. Now, I am going to bury them.

Carolyn and I pull the canoe up on the rocks at the island and I walk directly to where I left the bundles a year earlier and I find them under the bark beneath the blueberry bush. They've been chewed on by a mouse or squirrel, and tiny bits of red thread and white paper are scattered about on the moss, but the bundles are still mostly intact. Carolyn helps me look for a big rock. We wander around the island until we find one, and together we roll it back and I begin to dig beneath it, making a hollow for these bundles.

I dig and dig and dig, my fingernails filling with dirt. The whole time

I am digging, Carolyn is sitting beside me and I tell her about Anna. I tell her how the last time I talked to Anna she said that she didn't love me. I asked her if she loved me and this is what she said: "You might as well ask someone else that. Ask them, does Anna love Gretchen?" I asked her, didn't she care about me anymore? What about the tie between us, that powerful tether that would bind us together forever, and she said this: "What tie? I don't want that anymore. I only remember bad things when I think of you."

Of course it had started out differently. We had had good times in the short time we were together, like the ski trip we took to northern Minnesota. One night on that trip snow fell in flakes the size of cotton balls, and the woods were dark and sweet and little red lanterns set out by the owner of the resort we stayed at lit our way along the trails.

The lanterns made me feel as if I were inside the stories about Narnia that I'd read as a teenager, or inside the stories about Shangri-la, inside those stories about a secret safe place away from everything that could ever hurt me, or Anna, or anyone.

She and I stopped and leaned forward on our ski poles, breathing hard, our breath coming out in tiny puffs of steam. There was something in the woods then. And we didn't know whether to be afraid of it or to be happy, but mostly we were happy, and I kissed her and said, "It feels like anything is possible here, doesn't it?"

Later, at the cabin, I told Anna that I needed to do something to mark this time. It was a special anniversary. It was spring and it had been a year already since I had left Craig and moved into a new life. Only a year. A whole year. A yawning, spreading year and also the shortest year of my life so far. "What do you want to do?" she asked me, and I said I didn't know, but after dinner I dragged two sleeping bags and a candle out the cabin door and through the deep snow past the woodpile to the hard-packed ski trail. I spread the sleeping bags out and asked Anna to lie with me.

The candle would not stay lit. There were stars. She whispered to me, "What are we waiting for?" I told her I didn't know. I began to feel as if things were coming out of the woods and looking at us, that I could hear movement, breathing. I thought I heard footfalls. I tried to reason that I was hearing the blood in my veins coursing, moving the hairs in my ears. "Maybe it's just this," she said. "What?" I asked. "Maybe it's nothing, maybe it's just being here." She reached out and stroked my hand.

After we came in from the night and were standing brushing our teeth, she locked the door. We were in the middle of a northern Minnesota forest. No one was around except maybe a few people in the other resort cabins and the old couple who owned the lodge. But she was afraid. When we climbed into bed and snuggled into our sleeping bags I asked her, "Are you afraid?" I didn't tell her that if she had not locked the door I would have. Whatever I sensed in the woods she had too, and we both felt, vaguely, that it meant us harm.

She thought I was mocking her and she turned away from me and started to cry. A part of me saw her then only as pathetic. Her back shook with sobs. Curled up in the sleeping bag she looked like some thin baby bird. I felt helpless. I had never felt so mean. I had never wanted to hold someone so much. I had never felt love like that before.

I broke it off between us because, for one reason, she was married. But long after we left one another I kept writing letters to her. I was insistent. Even bothersome. I wanted something from her even though I wouldn't give her a thing.

In one letter I wrote: *I am looking out my apartment window to the yellow light coming from the stained glass across the way where workmen are plastering some new walls. It all looks orderly and hopeful.*

A friend asked me the other day if I grieved over Craig. "Yes," I said. "But not necessarily for him?" she asked. I thought for a moment and said, "Right. Not necessarily for him, but for what we had that was perfect and wonderful. For what I'll never have with someone else. For what is irreplaceable."

With you I felt enormous and beautiful. I didn't believe you when you said you loved me because you were so beautiful and perfect and complete. When I gave you flowers you received them so gracefully that you made everyone around you feel they had gotten them instead of you.

My friend says that now I have my work and that is good labor, as hard or harder than any love with another person. But I tell her, with Anna I became the person I want to be. I leapt into myself. It is not as if my rela-

tionship to my self can be separated from my love for her.

Being with you was being in a state of grace. I have called you an angel. My friend says this stuff, this magic, is in us and we don't always need other people to bring it out of us. She talks of certain religious practices through which you can also come to this place of grace. She tells me about practicing yoga—about the time when the Swami comes and touches you on the head and when he touches you, you experience enlightenment. This touch is meant to give you hope and focus and purpose, to show you where it is you are supposed to be going, to show you what grace feels like, so you will know what you are moving toward. But then the Swami leaves you and you do the rest yourself.

My friend says that maybe other people in our lives are like this, they awaken hopefulness in us, this focus and sense of purpose. They awaken us with love, and then the rest is labor, our labor. Eventually we come to the same state of grace ourselves, through our own persistence.

"She said she didn't love me," I tell Carolyn, and tears drip down into the muddy earth I am digging in. I feel Carolyn's hand in the center of my back. In that clear moment when I feel her hand, I also hear the words I just uttered repeated. I realize, as if I have been shocked with electricity, that this is not what Anna said at all. She didn't say "I don't love you." In fact, she never answered me. She turned the question back on me. In this crystalline second I see beyond everything, down into the roots of my life, her life, all of our lives, and I understand that I might as well have asked her, "Do you think I love myself?" And if I had asked her that, she would have said, "I don't know that. Only *you* know that."

The hole finally dug, I take each parcel and place it gently in the dirt, pushing hard to make sure it is in place. I tell Carolyn that the last time I spoke with Anna I asked her if I could be sure that she would carry me in her heart. I asked her if she would do me just one favor—keep the memory of me safe. She said no.

"She said no," I tell Carolyn. I didn't say it to Anna then, but I thought this: if Anna wouldn't do it, keep me safe, hold me close, even the memory of me, then who would? And again, I hear her voice echoing in the chamber in my head, and it is saying over and over again, "Do you love yourself? *Do* you? *Do* you? *Do* you?"

Carolyn helps me roll the rock back on top and I pack the sides with moss, so it looks as if nothing unusual has happened here. We heave the canoe off the rocks and paddle back to camp, paddling hard against the waves, trying to stay as much as possible in the lee of islands so that we don't get swept back out into the lake.

> 'Tis a gift to be simple,
> 'Tis a gift to be free,
> 'Tis a gift to come down
> Where you ought to be . . .

I am humming now, humming bits and pieces of all the songs that Carolyn and I have been singing all weekend. It is evening and our last night at Camp Van Vac. The five of us sit around the wood stove and tell stories. There are long moments of silence when we sit comfortably, with our legs stretched out, or bending forward with our arms resting on our knees, looking at the wood stove, at the cracks along the side of the door and at the small triangles in the grate in front where the fire shows through. There is nothing tangible that binds me to these women; no blood line, for instance, nothing visible. Only friendship. I am at home with them.

After what seems like hours, during which the air in the cabin grows so hot my face feels on fire and my head begins to spin just a little from sipping the last of the port, I go outside to get some air. I stand on the concrete steps of the cabin, listening, and off in the distance I hear a wolf howl. First the low notes rise, then they trail off into the night.

The cabin door opens and light comes flooding over my back, illuminating me from behind. It is Carolyn and I hold up my hand for her to stand still. She hears the wolf howl too. Then I point to the woods in front of us, where I hear faint skitterings and branches breaking. I ask her what that is, that soft sound. She looks at me with her most beautiful smile and she says, "The wind in the leaves," and then she smiles again and says, "The footsteps of mice," and then I say, "The breath of fish, the roots of mountains, the noise of cats as they move, the beards of women, the anguish of bears . . ."

Then the door opens again and everyone comes out and goes into the woods to empty their bladders before bed. There is laughing and the sounds of zippers being undone and done up again and then footsteps on the wooden stairs leading up to the bedrooms and someone raking the coals in the wood stove and then shutting the cast-iron door and the scrape of the damper being closed and then we call to each other, "Goodnight."

Gretchen Legler was born and raised in Salt Lake City, Utah, where she learned how to fish, backpack, climb mountains and ski. She moved to Minnesota in 1980 to attend Macalester College and began her relationship with the landscape of the Northwoods. Her writing career has included work as an agricultural journalist and feature writer for newspapers and magazines in Minnesota and North Dakota. She has a master's degree in creative writing from the University of Minnesota, where she also completed a Ph.D. dissertation on women nature writers. In 1992, she won a Pushcart Prize for her essay "Border Water." She currently teaches creative writing and English at the University of Alaska in Anchorage.

Her short stories and essays have appeared in the *Indiana Review*, *Grain*, *Hurricane Alice*, *The House on Via Gombito: Writing by North American Women Abroad* (New Rivers Press, 1991), *Uncommon Waters: Women Write About Fishing* (Seal Press, 1991), *Another Wilderness: New Outdoor Writing by Women* (Seal Press, 1994) and *A Different Angle: Fly Fishing Stories by Women* (Seal Press, 1995). *All the Powerful Invisible Things* is her first booklength work.